W9-AUU-130

John Lyons' The Making of a Perfect Horse

Communicating with Cues:

The Rider's Guide to Training and Problem Solving
Part III

ISBN: 1-879-620-58-8

Copyright© 1999 by Belvoir Publications, Inc., 75 Holly Hill Ln., Greenwich, Connecticut 06836. All rights reserved. No part of this publication may be reproduced, stored in a retrieval system, or transmitted, in any form or by any means, electronic, mechanical photocopying, recording, or otherwise, without the prior written permission of the publisher.

Please note: The information appearing in this publication is presented for educational purposes only. In no case shall the publishers or authors be held responsible for any use readers may choose to make, or not to make, of this information.

Belvoir Publications Inc.
Box 2626
75 Holly Hill Lane
Greenwich, CT 06836 USA

Lyons, John
Communicating with Cues:
The Rider's Guide to Training and Problem Solving Part III
John Lyons with Maureen Gallatin

ISBN: 1-879-620-58-8
1. Horses - Training   2. Horsemanship   3. Horses

Manufactured in the United States of America

John Lyons' The Making of a Perfect Horse

Communicating with Cues:

The Rider's Guide to Training and Problem Solving
Part III

John Lyons with Maureen Gallatin

Belvoir Publications, Inc.
Greenwich, CT

Contents

Sweet talking won't do it.

Carrots won't do it.

You need a cue!

Preface

If we were going to talk with someone from outer space who didn't know our language, and we couldn't speak his, we'd have to develop a language together. That's exactly what we're going to do in this book — develop a language we can use with our horse. It's a language we can safely use with our foals. We can use the same system to improve our adult horses' leading manners and to communicate better with our performance horses and trail buddies.

And, we're going to send all our signals down one rope — be it a lead rope or rein — as if the signals were traveling down a telephone line. We'll send a signal, then wait for a reply from our horse. When he responds correctly, we'll hang up the phone. When perfected, it may look like he's performing by remote control.

This book concentrates on the theme of "giving to the bit," which shows up in many forms. The principles apply whether there is literally a bit in the horse's mouth or not, and whether we are asking the horse to move his head or to move his hips. Just as the dancer doesn't dance by the whip, we don't communicate in a rough manner with our dance partners — our horses. Muscling a horse around or intimidating him isn't an option. We have a responsibility to treat our horses respectfully. When God made horses, He said they were good, and we agree. They are, after all, our perfect horses. God bless you, your family and your perfect horses.

John Lyons

All praise to the God and Father of our Lord Jesus Christ. He is the source of every mercy, and the God who comforts us. He comforts us in all our troubles so that we can comfort others.

2 Corinthians 1:3-4

Section I

Principles for
Ground Handling
Training
and
Problem Solving

1

You Ride The Horse You Lead

*If you can't control your horse from the ground,
you probably won't control him
from the saddle, either.*

The only thing more frustrating — and sometimes terrifying — than the horse who won't move forward at the speed and direction we want is the one who won't stop or slow down when we're riding him. Although we hate to admit it, if we have a control problem when we're riding, we probably have a lack of control on the lead line, too. So, let's deal with some of our riding problems while we're still safely on the ground.

Specifically what do we want?

First, we'll evaluate our expectations. What specific performance do we want from our horse, and how are we going to tell him what we want? Many of us make the mistake of being too vague in our requests, or we presume that the horse comes already equipped knowing what we want. For instance, we may assume that the horse should step briskly forward when we want him to and that when we pick up the lead rope, he should soften his neck, look at us to see what we want, and automatically slow his feet. But, horses aren't born knowing that's what we want of them. We need cues to help us communicate better.

If we have to rely on pulling his head one direction or another, we'll never be able to tell him to step forward, say, on the lunge line or onto the trailer, or even away from our feet. Most importantly, if

If you want your horse to confidently obey you when you ride, begin by teaching him good manners on the ground.

we don't have a cue to tell the horse that he did what we wanted, we'll never get him to repeat the performance. So, everything we want the horse to do relies on two cues — the "please" or request, and the "yes, you've got it" or the release. Also, we want our cues to be physical — not verbal or body language cues — because physical cues are stronger and more reliable. The object of this lesson is to teach the horse to go forward on cue and to give to pressure on the lead, which leads to him stopping on cue.

Developing a cue spot

You are going to tap the top of the horse's hip — the "go forward" cue spot — and stop tapping the moment the horse moves forward. Facing the horse's left shoulder, with your left hand hold the lead rope about two inches below the snap. The left hand merely controls the direction of the horse's head — not pulling the horse forward or preventing him from stepping back. Instead, it limits his head from swinging to the left or right. In your right hand, hold a stiff dressage whip.

John teaches Seattle the "go forward" cue by tapping on the cue spot on the top of his hip. Even though Seattle goes forward willingly, it's important to physically tap, so the horse makes a physical connection with that spot.

Here, Seattle is yielding to pressure on the lead. The bend in his neck is more than necessary for just walking forward, but John is taking the slack out of the line, preparing to ask Seattle to come toward him.

The reason for using a dressage whip, and not a buggy whip or some other type, is that a more flexible whip is harder to control. You should be precise when tapping, and more importantly, when stopping the taps the moment the horse does what we want him to do. And for safety reasons, it's important to use a whip that long. At no time do you want to find yourself behind the horse's front legs — you should stay forward, by the shoulder. Any farther back, you'll end up within kicking range of the hind feet.

Dressage whip in your right hand, facing the horse's left shoulder, with your left hand on the lead rope just below the halter ring, begin tapping a spot about the size of the palm of your hand, high on the horse's left hip. You are going to establish, in your mind and the horse's mind, a specific, physical cue spot. In fact, I mark it with a livestock paint marker or baby powder just to help me focus on one little place on the horse. Just as when you turn on the TV, pushing any old button on the remote won't do it; so, too, tapping any old place on the horse isn't specific enough.

We've chosen that spot, right upon the hip bone of the horse, because it is the place on the horse's rear least likely to elicit a kicking response. Any time you tap below the horse's stifle area (which is even with his belly), he's likely to kick. We don't want him to think that kicking is the correct response.

Who's the student here?

Learning this exercise takes longer than actually teaching it to the horse. Also, you have to set some boundaries for yourself. **You know the three basic rules of training: The trainer can't get hurt; the horse can't get hurt; and the horse should be calmer at the end of the lesson than at the beginning.** But beyond that, train yourself to focus on only one thing at a time. If you are trying to tell the horse to step one of his feet forward, and you expect him to isolate that behavior from whatever else he may be doing at the time you tell him he guessed the right answer, then you must do the same. If you are talking to the horse's feet, concentrate on the feet. That way, you'll be able to tell the horse, at exactly the right moment, that he did what you wanted.

Also, you'll have to recognize what is normal behavior and not get frustrated with the horse when things don't seem to go your way. For instance, our plan is to irritate the horse with the tapping, then to stop the irritation the moment he does what we want. The next time the horse becomes irritated in the same way, he'll try the same

If the horse gets distracted and ignores you on the lead rope, he's bound to do the same thing when you're riding — ignoring your rein requests and being insensitive to leg cues.

If the horse pushes into you, ignoring your space, he'll likely crowd between you and the trailer when you teach him to load, or knock into you with his shoulder as you lead him.

The horse who pulls back on the lead rope hasn't learned to give to pressure and is unsafe. He'll pull back when tied, or he'll tend to rear to relieve pressure from the reins.

response to see if he can get the irritation to end. So, if we begin tapping, then stop tapping when the horse backs up, what do you think he'll do the next time you begin tapping? You guessed it; he'll think that you want him to back up. Unless you really concentrate and are clear in your communication, you are likely to think that the horse is disobeying you, when in fact, he's trying his best to do what you want.

Another thing to keep in mind is that the right answer is always clearer to the teacher than to the student. **The horse will stumble onto the correct answer a number of times before he has really learned it.** So repeat the request and reward lots of times, to be sure he has the correct idea. Once he has the idea, then you want him to go beyond just that vague understanding to a conditioned response. That takes lots and lots of repetitions.

The horse will go through learning cycles — seeming to know the right response, then seeming to try every option other than the right response. When that happens, it's critical that you not change the cue or the reward — keep everything the same, and let him work through the ups and downs until his performance is consistent. Far from boring the horse, because you reward him each time he does what you want, you engage him in a game in which he (and you) win every few seconds. He doesn't mind playing then.

Going forward

Standing in position as we described, begin tapping the hip cue spot. Start tapping lightly at first, about two taps per second. The instant the horse moves forward, stop tapping. If the horse doesn't move forward after a few seconds, increase the intensity and frequency of the taps, putting the horse under more pressure. Don't increase it too fast, or you'll get too big a response from the horse. But neither do you want to stand there, tickling the horse for hours. Take a matter-of-fact approach.

If the horse steps back, walk with him and continue tapping. The moment he steps forward, stop tapping. If the horse steps left or right, keep tapping. If the horse stands there looking confused, the moment you think the horse is thinking about stepping forward, stop tapping. **Initially you can reward the horse's correct thought, to let him know he's on the right track.**

When the horse steps forward, allow him to walk just a few steps, then take the slack out of the lead rope, asking him to stop. Pet him generously. Because the idea is to develop a cue spot, we want to be able to repeat the "request" and "release," so we don't want the horse to walk long distances between requests.

Repeat the "go forward" cue 200 times on the left, tapping the horse's hip cue spot, then ceasing to tap the moment the horse steps forward. Then, teach the cue the same way on the right.

After you've done this exercise a few times, or with a more sensitive-type horse, you may find that the horse steps forward when you raise the whip, without being tapped. The purpose of this exercise is to establish a physical cue spot, so you must tap, but lightly.

THE OBJECT OF THIS LESSON IS TO TEACH THE HORSE TO GO FORWARD ON CUE AND TO GIVE TO PRESSURE ON THE LEAD LINE, WHICH LEADS TO HIM STOPPING ON CUE.

Stopping on the lead

Obviously, getting the horse moving is only half the equation; getting him to stop nicely is the other half. As with any exercise, first we get a response, then we fine-tune the response. When we discussed getting the horse to stop a few steps after giving him the "go forward" cue, we took all the slack out of the lead rope, pulling on it slightly. Then **we held that tension until the horse stopped or slowed his feet, at which time we released the lead.**

Now you want a better response. With the horse walking, take the slack out of the rope, pulling the rope either slightly toward you or back toward the horse's shoulder, depending on what the horse is doing. You don't want him to step on you, but you want him to soften his neck muscles and turn his nose toward you. When he does, release the rope.

Whenever a horse runs off, drags you off, pulls away from you or crowds into your space when you're leading him, he has stiffened his neck. He uses his neck for balance and leverage, and he stiffens the muscles in his neck so that he has power to fight us. We don't want him to "bully" us, so we want to be able to tell him to relax his neck muscles and turn his nose to us. (Incidentally, when his nose is toward us, his shoulder isn't smashing into us, either.)

So, no longer will you release the rope just because the horse's feet have stopped; you will make stopped feet and a softened neck prerequisites for the release. This will take some work, though, because the horse will get part of it right, then the other part. Keep in mind that the emphasis has changed; if the neck isn't soft, we are not releasing. In time, the horse learns the sequence of soft neck, then foot position. That will be critical to everything we do with our horse, particularly riding.

Building performance

Now that you've taught the cues in the "classroom," it's time to take the student out into the real world. Introduce a little excitement. If you are working on the "go forward" cue, for instance, how about asking him to go forward stepping onto a tarp or onto a sturdy log? Another horse in the area, or a little speed in the exercise, offers a chance to test how well conditioned the horse's response is. If he

There's no place for punishment in training a horse. If the horse doesn't understand what you want him to do, or if he doesn't do it, it's because the teacher hasn't broken the lesson down into steps small enough that the horse can comply.

responds well with no excitement around, but can't keep his mind on his job if another horse is working in the arena, that tells you that you have more work to do. Shorten the time between the requests, so that you become more insistent (in a polite, matter-of-fact way) than the distraction.

When he's a star with one other horse in the arena, try increasing the excitement level a bit more. For instance, try leading him down the driveway. The same horse who was rock solid in the arena may suddenly have a significantly stiffer neck. Or the horse who went forward with barely a touch of the whip in the arena may adamantly refuse to set one foot off his home turf. If he won't leave his friends and respond to your "go forward" cue with you on the ground, what do you think he's going to do when you try to take him on a trail ride alone?

From leading to riding

The same horse you lead is the one you will ride. There is no difference to the horse between the halter and bridle, or between the lead rope and the rein — it's all headgear to him. So, if you let your horse pull on the lead, it's guaranteed he will pull on the rein. If you accept a sluggish reaction to the "go forward" cue, you shouldn't be surprised when your horse ignores the "speed up" cue when you ride.

With that in mind, how can we use these two exercises to improve our horse's responsiveness under saddle? First, we can use them to train ourselves to isolate one response. By forcing ourselves, for instance, to wait for a soft neck, then stopped feet, before releasing the lead rope, we won't be distracted when our horse wanders all over the arena while we're teaching him to give to the bit. We won't be worrying about his feet — we'll only be focusing on the "give."

Counting 200 repetitions teaches us to focus, to notice the horse's reactions. If you notice that the horse does great through the 60s, but at 70 he seems resistant to the cue, you won't be surprised when, at 70 "gives" to the bit, the horse becomes resistant. However, knowing that at 85 he gets good again will encourage you to keep your training consistent.

Teaching the "go forward" and "yield to pressure" cues, and expecting increasingly better responsiveness, will get your horse in the habit of cooperating with you and looking for specific cues. He'll be in the habit of softening his neck and "giving to pressure," and he'll know that you are not going to release the rein until that happens.

Just for fun, think of what you wish your horse did better when you ride him. Is there any way to adapt this lesson to solve that problem? You can adapt these principles and exercises to solve many riding problems, because it's the same horse you ride that you lead.

What if you don't plan to ride this horse, but perhaps keep her as a broodmare or driving horse? The same compliance is important — especially for a driving horse. Beyond responsiveness, you'll find your partnership improving with your horse. The more you teach from the ground, the better your friendship and the easier and more fun it is to teach other lessons. ▣

2

Round Pen Pre-School

You know the right time to gain control
of your foal is when he's young and learning fast.
But can you "round pen" a little guy safely?

The youngest foal I ever worked in the round pen was three days old. But, the location — round pen or stall — isn't as important as what you do with your young horse. You say you are worried about adapting round-pen techniques to use with your foal because you are afraid for your foal's safety, his little legs and how his mom might react? We're concerned for your foal's safety, too, but that's precisely why round-pen principles are ideal for use with any horse — even a foal.

We look at round pens as classrooms and view horses as our students. But, the room isn't as important as treating your students right and making the subject matter understandable. Round-pen work is a subject similar to math — it can be extremely basic or very complex.

Good training principles will work with every horse, and foals are no exception. The lesson techniques or steps may change, but the principles don't. That's important to remember, because few horses are "textbook" cases, and training always involves figuring out what to do next. When I don't know what to do next with a horse, I review my basic training principles in order to develop the next steps in my lesson plan.

Round-pen work is just a series of training principles that allow us to gain control of a horse who hasn't been halter-trained. By developing control at a distance, we can keep our horse and ourselves safe as we teach additional lessons.

Setting the guidelines in place

You know the three rules we use to evaluate any training system, and any step in the training: The trainer can't get hurt, the horse can't get hurt, and the horse should be calmer at the end of the lesson than at the beginning. Let's see how those rules apply to working with foals or young horses.

First, a foal's little legs and lungs are developed well enough that he could run a short distance, to escape, for instance, if the herd were being attacked. But, they are not so well developed that you can treat him as you would an adult. **A foal — even a weanling — should never go more than the equivalent of two trips around a round pen without plenty of time to rest. Younger foals should go significantly less. You don't want to get the foal hot, excited or scared.**

Foals startle easily, so what may seem an acceptable move for you to make toward your riding horse may panic a foal or weanling. Their stopping mechanisms and coordination are not well developed, so once in motion, the foal doesn't have a very good sense of how to get himself stopped; thus, you see numerous crashes into

If you saw John working with a foal like this, would you assume he was doing round-pen work? Most people wouldn't. Round-pen techniques let you find a safe situation in which to begin getting along together and developing control.

Periodically reassure the mare, and spend some time petting her or grooming her. This lets the foal have time to think about what is happening and to get the message from his mom that you are an OK person to be around.

mom. But if mom isn't handy, you don't want to risk a crash into the fence or a feed trough.

Foals have short attention spans. So, for instance, when I work with a three-day-old foal, it may only be for two or three minutes at a time. As the foal matures, you can extend this. However, even when working with adult horses, mini-lessons work best. That's what happens each time we ask a horse to give to the bit, for instance. We teach him one mini-lesson. We may end up teaching 2,000 lessons in the course of a long trail ride, one at at time. That way the horse gets a reward each time he does what you've asked.

Folks often think that because a foal is small, they can muscle him around. When that happens, the foal learns to struggle and often gets free in the process, and the handler risks getting kicked or hit in the head with the foal's head. **We should treat a foal the same way we would a 1,000-pound horse, in that respect.**

When you can control a horse's movement, you can control the horse. And, when we can control the horse, we can keep him safe. So, just as with working an adult, we are going to begin by getting our foal's feet to move.

The round-pen principle we'll use is: **"First get his feet to move. Then get them to move consistently. Then move in the direction we want." Feet moving and running are not the same thing. No part of round-pen work, for either adult horses or babies, requires them to run around the pen.** In fact, the less energy they expend, the further you can take the training in any one session, because they then have enough energy to keep learning.

Everyone who's ever owned a mare and foal knows what happens when you want to pet the foal. You approach on the mare's left side, and the foal steps around behind the mare. That's the first part of round-pen work — the foal's feet moved. It didn't take being in a round pen, and it sure didn't involve running the foal around.

Beginning the training

Kentucky Horse Park generously offered to let John work with a pony foal only several days old, so we could show you how it's done. This foal had never had a halter on or had his feet handled, so everything John did was new to him. What wasn't new was lots of petting, which is what you'll want to do with your foal along with other training.

This foal is moving back toward his mom but under John's direction. He won't realize that John is controlling his movements until later in the lesson.

John tied the mare (after being told she had been taught to stand tied) to a fence post inside a secure pasture. After waiting a few minutes for the mare and foal to relax, John walked along the fence line over to the right side of the mare. The foal went around to the mare's left side. John's first goal had been accomplished — he got the foal's feet to move.

You can probably guess what happened next. John went around to the left side of the mare, and the foal circled around behind mom to get to her other side. With just a few repetitions, goal No. 2 was met — the horse's feet were moving consistently.

Now some people might think that by doing this you'd be teaching the horse to go away from you. If you quit at this point, they may be right. But, until you can tell the feet to move, you can't tell them where to move.

Getting specific

When we worked the adult horse in the round pen, we didn't just generically tell the horse to move. We were very specific, focusing on the horse's left hip and developing that as a cue spot to tell him to move forward to the left. So, too, we'll establish the hip as a cue spot with our foal.

John looks at the top of the foal's left hip as he kisses to the foal, and his body language tells the foal to move away. If the foal doesn't move off, John raises his hands as if to gently "shoo" the foal away, still focusing on the hip.

When the foal moves a step or two, John "backs off," relaxing his body posture, which tells the foal he did the right thing and ends one mini-lesson. After a moment, John again focuses on the left hip cue spot, telling the foal to move forward. As you can imagine, the foal won't go too far from the mare. Before long, John will have the foal making a circle (it will probably be only about 15 feet in diameter) back to mom. John now does the same thing from the right, teaching the foal to go forward from the right hip cue spot.

There may be a time, that instead of making a circle, the foal thinks doubling back is the shortest route back to mom. Here's where the foal will get the first inclination that John is controlling his movements: John will step forward, essentially using his body language to block the foal's shoulder. When the foal pauses, John will then drop back so he can cue the foal's hip forward and continue the circle. This redirection takes careful use of body language. At no point do you want to frighten the foal or cause him to run into the fence. **Just as**

John focuses on the foal's left hip cue spot, as he kisses to him and encourages the foal to move. Notice that the body language — of both John and the foal — is very relaxed.

John is working on asking the foal to turn to his left. The foal's natural inclination is to go to the right, toward his mom. But, John is blocking that path and gently encouraging the foal to turn to the "outside" and go back to mom the long way.

when working with mature horses, if there is any possibility of the horse running into the trainer or into the fence, back off and allow the horse to pass.

If the foal gets to feeling brave or playful, and decides to scoot away from the mare, just be patient and wait for the foal to return, or go out to where the foal is and use that as an occasion to tell the foal to go forward, back toward mom.

This takes an amazingly short amount of time, and you'll be teaching your foal that **the kiss means to move**; but, more importantly, you are teaching the foal that you can control him without causing him pain — emotional or physical. That's how trust is developed.

Changing direction

Once the foal is moving forward on cue and you are able to get him to circle, then you'll want to teach him to change directions on cue. Just as with the big horses, the easiest way is to block his path, then immediately step away when he's made the turn. Because foals can be so reactive, be sure to allow plenty of room. Don't suddenly step toward the foal's path or crowd him into the fence.

So, step about 20 feet in front of him along the fence. When you can get him to change directions fairly consistently, then you'll want to begin to shorten the distance he travels between changes of direction, until he only travels about 10 feet before you ask him to change. Eventually he'll stop, standing near the fence. When he does, step away from him and let him just stand there and relax. Reassure him with your voice.

Both eyes, please

Your next objective is to get the foal to look at you with both eyes. This is the foundation for teaching the horse to come to you when called. With the foal standing parallel to the fence (you may have to use a series of stops and starts to get him there), walk over to the fence about 15 feet in front of him and just stand there, making it easy for him to look at you. After just a few moments, walk away. That lets him know that was all you wanted.

Walk back to the fence again, and again just stand there, this time a little longer. If the foal begins to look away, kiss to him. When he looks at you for a moment, walk away, releasing him, as it were, from the cue.

If, while you are standing in front of him, the foal begins to back up or move away (which he may, if he's thinking you want him to move or if he's worried about you), then just step toward the center of the pen, and ask him to step forward. **You don't want any "backward" thoughts in your foal's mind.** Once he's stepped forward, again walk to a place on the fence way out in front of him, kiss to him, and just stand there. If he doesn't look at you within two seconds, again step toward the middle of the pen and ask the foal to step forward. Repeat this step until when you kiss to him, the foal looks at you. You'll want to do this from both sides, so the foal gets used to looking at you when the fence is on his left as well as when it's on his right, and eventually when he's not near a fence at all.

Round-pen review

So, we've achieved many of our round-pen objectives: Neither we nor our foal were injured. Our foal should be calmer around us at the end than at the beginning. Our foal's feet are moving, moving consistently, and moving in the direction we want. With practice, our foal will go forward from the left and the right, turn to the left or the right, stop parallel to the fence and look at us with both eyes.

Everyday training

One consideration, though, is not to "undo" the training by backing away from your foal. Sometimes foals get pretty frisky, and owners get afraid the foal will kick them or bang into them, so the positions get reversed: The foal learns he can control the owner's movements. So, for instance, in the stall, tell your foal to move over one step if he gets too pushy. Don't move to get out of his way.

Be sure that your training is consistent. The foal can't differentiate between a training session and normal farm activities. His little computer is taking in data all the time, and he's learning from it. So your body language any time you are with the foal should reassure him when he's doing what you want, or control his movements to make sure that he does what you want. That's how to keep you both safe.

This entire teaching process should be a positive experience for both you and the foal. Make it reassuring, with lots of petting, so your foal develops confidence in you and your leadership. ■PH

3

Basic Training For Foals

Horses aren't born knowing what behavior
is appropriate, and there's no better time
to teach them than when they are young.

At nearly every symposium or clinic I'm asked the same question: "Do I treat a foal the same way as I do an adult horse?" The answer is both yes and no. "Yes," in that I don't allow my foal to do anything **I wouldn't allow a 2,000-pound draft horse to do.** "No," in that I take special consideration to allow for the foal's more fragile physical condition, the fact he can frighten easily and so forth. But I do not compromise on what I consider acceptable behavior.

Foals grow strong quickly, and before you know it, they are hard to handle. The same foal you could muscle around at two days of age will drag you across the corral when he gets bigger. So, I'm careful to avoid even inadvertently teaching my foal anything that I don't want, and I work to teach him what behavior I do want.

For instance, you may think it's cute when the foal comes dashing toward you, but you'll be appalled to find your big horse crashing into you and invading your space. If you lead your foal by pulling him around, you'll end up spending a lifetime dragging your horse behind you. Worse yet, the lead rope to the horse is no different from the reins, so if you teach him to drag on the lead, you'll essentially teach him to pull on the reins.

Sweet little nibbles can quickly become biting behavior. Then there's the matter of allowing you to handle his body. If we allow a foal to pull his leg away, he'll end up having trouble with the farrier later in life. The same applies to clipping ears, examining his mouth

Hugging can be part of the sacking-out process. The horse learns that he can be handled — and restrained — without it causing him any pain. It also helps build his confidence and trust in the trainer.

and so forth. And, should the foal need handling, say, for trailering or treating a wound, then we'll risk injury by having to force him into being handled.

What sacking out teaches the foal

On my ranch, we begin the sacking-out process right away. We pet him and love on him, so he gets comfortable with people handling his whole body. We pet him everywhere, including putting our fingers in his mouth and handling his ears. And we pick up his feet.

In fact, at home we have a rule: You're not allowed to pet the foal unless you pick up all four feet. And, since everyone comes to see the new foal, he gets his feet picked up lots of times a day.

Sacking out is really the process of exposing the foal to an object, but withdrawing the object before he gets worried enough about it that he feels he has to move. **The foal learns that being petted or groomed not only doesn't hurt him, but it feels good. He learns he doesn't have to bolt at every new scary object, and he gets better at handling his emotions.**

Beginning sacking out

Just as with adult horses, the first object we sack our foal out with is our hand. One difference between sacking out and ordinary petting is knowing when to stop petting.

If we pet the horse and he moves away while we're petting him, he learns that when he doesn't feel like being handled, he can move away. He's the one in control. We want to reverse that. We want to teach him to stand for handling, but that we are not going to overwhelm him. Eventually he'll learn to stand for grooming no matter how long the handler wants him to — but that's the goal, not the starting place.

To begin, we'll pet the foal, but stop petting before we think he wants to move away. So, if we think he'll pull his head away, for instance, in three seconds, stop petting him in two.

Pet him just a few strokes at a time. Then, we'll work up to resting our hand on the foal, more strokes and so forth. I do a lot of petting on a horse's head, especially if he's a colt. So, I'll pet the neck or shoulder, then go back to petting his head. Pet down his leg, then back to the head and so forth.

Each time we pet the horse, we stop petting before we feel the foal will move away from us. This is extremely important. If you misgauge it and the foal moves away, do not attempt to contain him, and do not "chase" him. Learning is a cumulative process, and one or two "escapes" aren't going to ruin anything. Consistency is the key.

If the foal does step away from you, use your kiss cue to tell the foal to look at you with both eyes. When he does, just relax, letting him know he did the right thing. Begin the lesson again.

This same thing will happen when you are holding or handling his head. He may try to pull his head away from you, like a little child who doesn't want his nose wiped. When that happens, there are two options. If he's just tensing his neck and you think by continuing to hold him a moment longer that he'll relax it again, then do that. As soon as he relaxes his neck even a smidge, release him.

If he actually pulls away from you, call him back using your kiss cue. Don't "chase" his head, any more than you'd chase his feet if he moved his whole body away from you. You don't want to set up a confrontation; you want to establish control without conflict.

If the foal pulls away repeatedly, you are pushing him too fast. Drop back in the lesson so you can release him before he pulls away.

Once the foal is comfortable with your hand petting him, pet him with an object, such as a washcloth. When he accepts the washcloth, try using a soft brush, then a lead rope without a snap. Work up to a towel, burlap sack and plastic bag, each time remembering to withdraw the object before the foal moves away.

With this method, he gets used to the object, but more importantly, you teach him that he can get worried about a new object without having to move his feet, because you are not going to over-scare him. It's the beginning of developing emotional control. You are essentially training him to give you time before he moves away. In return, you don't violate his trust — you control him without causing him pain.

Now to the feet

When we are ready to pick up his feet, we'll start out by petting his shoulder, then moving back to pet his head, as we've been doing. Then we'll move down his leg to pet above his knee, always removing our hand before we think he'll move away.

Finally, when we can pet down around his ankle, we can nudge him gently so his weight leans on the other front foot. When he's relaxed about that, pet the foot — but stop petting before he tries to move it. Return to petting his head.

Rather than try to chase the foal's head to put the halter on, John kisses to the foal to teach him to drop his head and all but halter himself.

When we're ready to pick up the foot, we won't squeeze his tendon or do anything that will cause him discomfort; instead, with his weight resting mostly on, say, his right front foot, we'll gently grasp around his left front ankle and pick up the foot for a second, holding it close to the ground. We'll release it, of course setting it gently on the ground a moment later, and return to petting the foal's head.

Work your way down the horse's leg and back on his body, each time returning to his head. Be sure you stand as far forward as you can while working with him. It's not uncommon for foals to kick as you get to the back end, and even a foal's kick can cause serious injury.

By the time you are ready to pick up the back feet, the foal knows the pattern and feels secure with what you are going to do, though having his back feet picked up will be a new sensation for him.

Preparing for the halter

For all of the horse's life, he'll be expected to stand quietly for haltering, so there's no reason to rush this lesson. Take the time to teach him correctly when he's little, and he'll work willingly with you his whole life.

By the time I'm ready to halter-train a foal, I've already handled him extensively and sacked him out, and I can control where his feet are going by using my body language and specific cues. I've petted him with at least 50 objects, so adding another new object — a halter — isn't any big deal. I'll pet the foal with the halter, including all over his head.

Drape the halter over one of his ears, then remove it and pet him. Do the same with the other ear a number of times, then slowly slide it up over his muzzle. (You've probably done this with the lead rope prior to now as part of ordinary sacking out.)

Once he's completely comfortable with all that, teach him to drop his nose into the halter. Stand to the side, as you see me doing in the photos, and hold the halter a few inches below his nose and to the side. Begin kissing to him. Keep kissing (softly) until he begins to move his nose toward the halter. Immediately stop kissing. The foal has already learned that the kiss means "move something." Now you are teaching him that another cue usually accompanies a kiss, so he should move a specific part of his body. He'll learn that when you have the halter in place and kiss to him, you want him to drop his nose into the hole.

When he moves his nose toward the halter, stop kissing and praise him. Don't "capture" his head with the halter, but let him know all

By the time we're ready to buckle the halter, the foal has had the halter on and off about 50 times. He's learned to stand quietly and not pull away from the handler.

you wanted was for him to move his nose toward it. After a number of repetitions, you can begin sliding the halter on. After you feel sure that the foal is comfortable with the halter on for more extended periods, buckle the halter, pet the foal, then unbuckle it and take it off. Do these movements slowly but matter-of-factly so the foal doesn't get frightened. With repetition, you can move faster, still without being rough.

Incidentally, you can do these same exercises with any age horse. So, if your horse is hard to halter or reluctant about having his feet or ears handled, use the same lesson. ◼PH◼

4

Don't Drag Me Off!

*It doesn't matter if you are leading
your horse or riding him — any step he takes
without your consent is a running-away step.*

When you lead your horse, do you get dragged along like a skier at the end of a tow rope? Would you like to improve your horse's leading manners and also be at least 25 percent safer on your next trail ride? Twenty-five percent is a big improvement, and an investment of just 15 minutes now and then will do it for you — on any horse.

Getting to a stop

It does no good for the engineer to put on the brakes at the front of the train if the rest of the train keeps pushing it forward. **So, too, no matter how severe a bit you put in the horse's mouth or how much pressure you put on the bit, if you can't stop the back end of the horse, stopping his mouth won't help much.**

We all know that a horse can continue running straight ahead even with his head turned to the side. That's because the most powerful part of the horse — his hip — pushes him along. So, before we can get the whole horse to stop, we have to prevent the hip from pushing the horse forward. We can do this by asking the horse's hip to step to the side. It then loses forward-pushing power, and we gain control of the horse's movement. But, while the hips are the powerhouse, it's often the horse's left shoulder that knocks into the person "leading" him. We'll show you how to control both.

This horse's right shoulder is running away, but it's gotten a big push forward from the horse's hips. If John can get the hip to move over, then the shoulder can stop.

Establish an objective

We have to be able to communicate what we want our horse to do, and anyone who's tried to power a horse around on a lead rope knows that the horse is considerably stronger than they are. So, that's where folks often turn to using some kind of pain-inducing mechanism, such as a chain shank over the horse's nose. What that essentially does is cause the horse pain when he pulls on the rope. It is effective sometimes in telling the horse what not to do, but unfortunately, it doesn't tell the horse what to do. And, if the horse's fear or excitement level is stronger than his fear of the pain of the chain shank, then he'll pull on that shank and keep on going.

So, gaining control first of all requires a plan. **The plan we're going to use is to teach the horse that when he feels pressure on the lead rope, he should "follow" the pull.** We call that "yielding to pressure." So, for instance, the horse who pulls back when he is tied doesn't move toward the lead rope — he pulls against it. The horse who drags the handler off when being led doesn't relax his neck and move his jaw toward the handler — he stiffens his neck and pulls the other way.

Yield to pressure

Most leading lessons presume that when you pick up the lead rope, your horse knows to "give" to the rope and relax his neck. To teach him to yield to pressure, ask the horse to walk forward in a circle as you lead him. Put a small amount of pressure on the lead. When he relaxes his neck, turning his nose slightly toward you, release the rope. Until he turns his nose slightly toward you, keep pressure on the lead rope. With repetition, he'll learn that the response you want when he feels pressure is to move toward the source of the pressure. If you get an unwanted response when you put pressure on the rope (like him throwing his head up or stiffening his neck), you are using too much pressure for this stage of the lesson.

How to begin

While teaching the horse to yield to pressure as we described above is the ideal, it's hard to do if the horse is dragging you around. You then have a "which came first, the chicken or the egg?" situation. You can't just hang on until the horse "gives," if he has no motivation to give, as we described earlier. So, as for anything you want your horse to do, you have to have a motivator. If the horse was heading north, do you think he'd have more power if he could head straight north, or if he had to go north one step, then west two steps, then north, then west two steps, then south, then north? Obviously, the more times you interrupt his "northerly" direction, the less steam he'll have to drag you to the north with him.

We're going to approach this leading problem in two ways. The first is from the horse's hip. We'll give you the gist of how that works, but then we'll take you through a detailed lesson in the next chapter. In this chapter, we'll teach you two ways to control the horse's shoulder. With the horse who is really excited and out of control, hip control may be the first step, and as you'll see, it is also one way to set up to control the shoulder. But, many horses are just a bit rude, and we need a simple means of telling them to not invade our space and to not pull on the lead rope. And since we can't tell the horse what "not" to do, we'll have to teach him what we want.

The pushy shoulder

The rude horse, the one who just stands a little too close or isn't very respectful of your space could benefit from this exercise, but you'll need to control the hip of the horse who is radically out of control. To deal with a pushy shoulder problem you are going to "connect" the lead rope to the horse's shoulder. With the horse standing still, take all the slack out of the lead rope, pulling it back as if you are trying to connect it with the point of the horse's shoulder, as you see me doing in the photos. Keep pulling until the horse brings his nose slightly toward that spot and relaxes the pull on the lead rope slightly. Pet him generously. He may or may not take a step back.

This time, ask the horse to walk and, before he gets walking too energetically, pull the rope back toward the point of the shoulder again. Again, release when he "gives" with his head and neck and the shoulder stops pushing forward.

What you are trying to do is introduce to the horse the idea that there is a release available. You don't want to be in a pulling contest long term, but it may require holding the rope steadily while

John pulls the lead rope toward a point on the horse's shoulder.

Sometimes it requires strength to hold against a pulling horse. But, we only want the horse to get a release when he moves his head toward his shoulder.

the horse pulls hard against you. Make sure that you don't pull against his pull. By that I mean, you are looking for the place to release. When he moves his head even a smidge in the desired direction, don't continue to pull, but release the lead rope.

Teaching the hip

To start the lesson: Put a halter, or full cheek snaffle bridle, on your horse. If you are using a bridle — which is a good idea with a horse who pulls away from you — snap the lead rope to the left ring of the bit. (Just be sure that when you take the slack out of your lead rope, you do so steadily. Don't jerk on the bit.)

Standing by the horse's left shoulder, ask him to walk forward, using the "go forward" cue (tap the top of the horse's hip with a stiff dressage whip, and stop tapping as soon as he moves forward). When he is moving in a circle around you freely and not trying to stop on his own, take all the slack out of the rein or lead rope, pulling it toward you or back toward the horse's withers, turning his head toward you. Continue pulling on the rope until his right hind foot steps to the right or the left hind foot crosses in front of the right. When he does either, release the rein or rope, and pet the horse.

Initially, the horse may take only one step over. When he does, immediately release the rein and pet him, then repeat the lesson. Once he's pretty consistently taking one step, continue to hold tension on the rein or lead until he takes a second step. Then release. He'll get the idea that you want two steps. At first, it may require a fair amount of pull, but as the horse learns, you should be able to get the same response with lighter and lighter signals, as long as the horse is walking forward freely when you ask for the sideways step. After each release, wait for the horse to stop or relax a bit before asking him to walk forward again.

While this first part of the exercise allows you to break the horse's forward push, it doesn't stop the horse. But, as you practice moving the hip over, you'll observe an interesting phenomenon: Let's say you are working with the left rein and asking the horse's hips to step over to his right. Assuming you have him walking briskly, then ask him to step over; he'll take fairly good-sized steps. As he takes the second step to the right with his back feet, the horse will balance momentarily on his left front leg, and his left shoulder will stop moving. Now you have two major parts under control; you've stopped the hip from pushing the shoulders forward, and you've stopped one front foot.

A freebie: the shoulder

As we said earlier, when the horse's hips step far enough to the right on cue, his left shoulder will stop as he pivots on his left front foot. When this happens, release the rein again. As you'll find out when you work through the lesson, there will be times that the horse's hips move over, but his left front foot keeps moving, too. Accept that at first and release the rein, because initially you are talking only to the hip. Since you can only talk to one part of the horse's body at a time, get the hip doing what you want first.

Now, if it happens that the horse stops his left shoulder and pivots on that foot right away, he's given you a freebie. Although nothing you actually did made the shoulder stop, reward the horse when it happens. That will tell him to stop his shoulder when he swings his hips to the side. He'll recognize the pattern, and eventually when you pick up the lead — thinking about the hips moving, then the shoulder stopping — both will happen.

Lighter and lighter

We all want our horses to respond to a light signal. Obviously, then, we need to use a light signal in our training. For a horse to respond lightly, he must have energy in his body. That energy comes from forward movement. So, make sure the horse walks forward with energy, or he can't step his hindquarters energetically over.

Once your horse has energy, start making your signal lighter and lighter, to teach him to respond to a more subtle cue. To do that, move your hands slower, giving him time to respond. If he doesn't respond, however, you'll be forced to ask him to step more lively.

Think about it: If a horse doesn't respond to a light signal, doesn't it make sense to go to a stronger signal? No. You won't get a horse responding to a light signal by using a stronger one, any more than

No longer fighting, this horse is responsive to the lead rope and his neck is soft. John asks his hind end to take two steps to the right. Note that the horse is balancing on his left front leg.

you'll get him more responsive to the bridle by using leg cues. Once you've taken the slack out of the lead rope (which may mean you are pulling on the rope), you don't need to pull any harder; instead, ask the horse to step more lively. He may end up pulling pretty hard against you, but if you hold your position steady, he'll end up putting his motion into the direction you want.

You'll be amazed how using these techniques will help control a distracted or disrespectful horse quickly. No longer will you have to put up with your horse dragging you off at the end of a lead rope. When you can control the horse, you can keep both him and yourself safe. And, safety is the first step in enjoying working with our horses. ▣

5

Control That Hip

Gaining control of the horse's hip is the single-most important thing you can do to gain control of the horse. This one lesson, if thoroughly taught, can prevent a runaway, as well as help assure your safety on the ground.

"Connecting the rein to the hip" may be the most important lesson you ever teach yourself — and your horse. One of our key training principles is that if we can control one part of the horse, we can control the whole horse. For instance, **when we deal with the horse who rears, we control the tip of his ear. When we tell the ear to go down, his head (and front feet) can't go up at the same time.** So, focusing on one part of the horse at a time, what part is the powerhouse in the following situations?

1. A horse who runs straight ahead with his rider, despite the rider having turned the horse's head.
2. A horse whose front feet are off the ground as he springs away from his handler.
3. A horse who is about to lift off over a jump.
4. A horse who cowkicks at the person attempting to mount.

If you answered, "the horse's hip," to all of the above, you would be right.

The hip moves the horse

Remember back to when we first worked in the round pen? We focused on gaining control of the horse's hip — telling the hip to move (the horse) forward. Now, assume for a moment that you are standing

Try this exercise for some fun and insight into how the hip controls the horse. In these photos, assume that the first person represents the horse's nose and neck, the second person is the body, and John represents the horse's hip. Even if the horse's head is turned to the side, the body cannot turn because the hip pushes the body straight ahead.

ready to mount your horse, and you feel him about to kick you. What would you do instinctively? You'd either shove his hindquarters away or pull his head toward you, so that his hindquarters would step away. That's the concept we'll use — we'll develop a cue to tell the horse's hips to move over — so he can't kick, launch himself forward, or run off with us.

Whenever you want the horse to do something on cue, ask yourself four questions. **What part of the horse do you want to move? Then, in what direction do you want it to move? Third, what is the motivator — what will cause the horse to do this the first time? Finally, what is your "yes answer" cue?** In other words, how will you tell the horse that he did what you wanted?

Well, in this lesson, we already know we want to control the hip and we want it to move to the side. Now, how do we get that done, consistently?

Speak the right language

Let's review the language we use to teach the horse what we want him to do.

■ When we taught the horse the "calm down" cue, otherwise known as the rear-ending lesson, we put pressure on the rein, held pressure on it until the horse's head went down, then released the pressure.

■ When we teach the horse to give to the bit, we take all the slack out of the rein, while thinking about the horse moving his nose to the side, then hold pressure on the rein until he "gives" his head to the side.

■ When we taught the "go forward" cue, we tapped on the horse's hip continuously until he moved one of his feet forward. Then we stopped tapping.

We'll use the same language — cue the horse; continue cueing until the horse responds; then release the horse from the cue. The motivator we'll use is tension on the rein, or lead rope. And the "yes answer" cue is the release from that tension. Let's put our training principles into action.

Go forward

Everything we want our horse to do, even turning and stopping, involves movement. So, our first objective is to get the horse moving. Facing the horse's left shoulder, with the lead rope in our left hand, tap high on the horse's left hip with a stiff dressage whip. (This is the same cue we used when teaching him to step forward for trailer loading, for leading exercises, lungeing and for the WESN lesson.)

As soon as he moves one of his feet forward, stop tapping. Back to the four questions for a moment: Answer one, we want to control the hip. Answer two, we want it to move the horse forward. Answer three, the motivator is the tap of the dressage whip. Answer four, the "yes answer" cue is that we stop tapping with the whip.

So we use our language to get the hip moving the first direction — forward. If the horse moves any direction but forward, we keep tapping until he takes a step forward.

Now, if our horse is running away with us, we do not want the hip pushing the horse forward. But **we don't have a "not forward" cue. And, we can't effectively tell our horse "don't" do something — instead, we must tell him what we do want him to do.** So, if

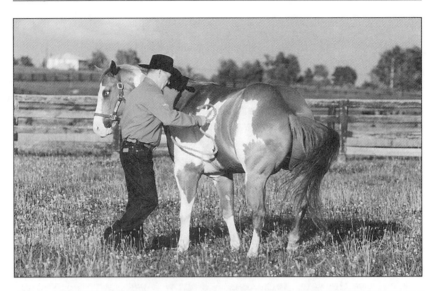

At first, the lesson may be awkward. If the horse is too close to you, you'll have to be careful not to get stepped on. In the top photo, John is holding the lead right below the halter; that way, he can keep tension on it until the horse's hips begin to move over. It may be easier to start this horse on a lunge line instead of a lead line, as he is doing with Seattle in the bottom photo. He has allowed Seattle to walk past him; then, without jerking, he has applied pressure to the lead. You can see how easily Seattle could step his hips to the right and get John to release the rope.

the hip is already pushing the horse forward, we have to give it a different job.

There are only six directions in which we can ask any body part to move — forward, back, up, down, left and right. It's probably unrealistic to try to go from forward to backward, and we don't want the hip to go up or down (then we'd really have a rough ride). If we are on the left side of the horse, it's unlikely we want the hips to come to the left, so we'll develop a cue to tell the hips to move right.

Our horse is now walking in a circle around us. Holding the rein or lead rope about three to four feet from the horse's head, put pressure on the lead — pulling it toward you. Hold pressure on the rope until you see the horse's right hind foot step to the right, or the left hind foot cross in front of the right. Either way, the hindquarters move right.

As soon as you see that happening, release the lead rope. Our final objective is for our horse to take two steps over — one with each hind leg — when we pull on the lead as we focus on the horse's hip. We won't expect two steps at first, but we'll reward progress in that direction.

This is one of those exercises that makes more sense when you do it than when you read it. To make things easier, put a mark on the top of your horse's hip (perhaps with baby powder or with a livestock paint marker). Train yourself to keep focusing on that cue

Don't be surprised if the horse pulls pretty hard against you and hanging onto that rope occasionally requires some strength. Here John works to get the horse to move his hips over for the first time; then he can release the rein and tell the horse he did the right thing.

spot. When that spot moves to the horse's right, release the rope. When the spot isn't moving to the horse's right, keep tension on the rope. It's as simple as that. Actually, screening out everything else is the difficult part. It's not important where his front feet are going, or if his head is up or down. You can fine-tune the response later, but for now, just focus on the hip.

What if the horse just walks toward you, but doesn't move his hips over? Start a little farther from him, as if you were lungeing him. Wait until his shoulder passes you, so he has to turn his hips away in order to turn his nose toward you. Then work to get the same response on a progressively shorter line.

What if, instead of the horse's hip moving over, the horse pushes his shoulder into you? Keep pressure on the lead rope, walking into the horse if necessary. It doesn't really matter what direction you pull the rope. It's an awkward dance at first, but with practice you'll find it falling into place.

Benefits, benefits, benefits

So what can you do with this lesson? Amazing things. It really is a safety-valve type of operation. What if you are invited to ride some-one else's horse on a trail ride? You can't spend hours teaching him to give to the bit before the ride. But, you can spend 10 minutes making sure you can move his hips over. If the horse should try to run off, you can change his direction by moving his hips over. If you can change his direction, you'll find that you can stop him.

What if, one windy morning, your horse feels like he's about to buck? Move his hips over. He has to stiffen his neck somewhat in order to buck, and that's hard to do if you have his head turned to the side. He'll also have a hard time powering off his hindquarters if you have him doing the two-step.

What if you have to lead a difficult horse? You can't outpull him, but you can get him to move his hips over once. And if you can do it once, you can move them over again and again. You'll find that when you move the horse's hips over far enough, say, to the right, his left front foot will stop for a moment.

And, we can fine-tune the signals and use this same lesson to speak to other parts of the horse's body. You'll be amazed how one little lesson can be such a handy tool. ᴘʜ

Section II

Principles For Teaching
Your Horse
To Give To The Bit

6

Understanding Giving

*Have you heard the terms "giving to the bit"
and "connect the rein to the feet" and wondered
what we were talking about? Well ...*

If you are going down the trail and having trouble with your horse, it is not his attention you need, it is his performance. You will eventually get his attention, but it comes after other things. First comes the *rider's* concentration, then the *rider's* consistency, then the *horse's* performance, and finally the *horse's* attention.

But how do you get his performance? You teach the horse to give to the bit. This one exercise will enable you to stop your horse from rearing, being barn sour or jigging on the trail, and will be what you'll use even to teach the horse to lie down. Once you and your horse have learned it, you will be amazed at how effective it is. But, while the exercise isn't complicated, being consistent with it is difficult.

At my three-day clinics, I spend a great deal of time talking this subject through. In fact, we spend an entire morning in a classroom session discussing exactly what I'm going to tell you now in a few pages. Then, we spend the next 2 1/2 days putting it into practice.

I'll tell you an amazing fact: If you concentrate on teaching the horse one thing, any one thing, you'll eventually get the whole horse's attention. The one thing I find most effective to teach the horse is to "give" to the bit. While "giving to the bit" can mean different things, it's a phrase I use in a very specific manner. **It means that when I pick up on the rein and take all the slack out of the rein, asking the horse to move a specific part of his body, he responds with energy, moving that part in the direction I've asked.**

Let's look at an example. Say you dangled the keys to your new car in front of your house-bound teenager. If he got off the sofa and said, "Oh, well, OK Dad, if you insist" (the way he does when you ask him to clean up his room), that would not be considered "giving." But, if he jumped off the sofa to grab the keys enthusiastically, we would say he was "giving to the keys." Since we can't motivate our horse with keys, we find something he cares about as much as that teen cared about the car keys.

The horse does not want you to pull on the reins. He'll do anything rather than have that happen. So that's the motivation we'll use. We'll slowly take the slack out of one rein, thinking about what we want him to do. When we've taken the time to teach him our riding language, he'll understand what we want and he'll do what we want, in order that we release his rein — like, perhaps, that teenager cleaned his room in order to get Dad to give him the car keys. We can use one rein to talk to any part of the horse's body. It's a concept that the horse understands quicker than we do. So, for the sake of discussion, let's consider the rein to be like a telephone.

Calling our horse

We can use the same phone to call any number of businesses. We can even call just to check up on a friend — we don't need a separate phone for each person we call. The phone analogy applies to working with our horse. **We can use the same bit and rein to talk with any part of our horse — we don't need different aids to talk with different parts of his body.** I'll explain how it works.

Let's say you were planning to remodel a house and want to talk with various suppliers. Thumbing through the Yellow Pages, you find the plumber, the kitchen cabinet shop, the wallpaper store and the carpet center. You dial the plumber, and he agrees to do the job; then you hang up. With the same phone, you then call the kitchen cabinet shop and arrange for samples of cabinet finishes. This time, you don't hang up the phone; but, with the receiver in your left hand, your right hand pushes down the big button, and voila! — you have a dial tone — ready to call wallpaper supply. You can call any phone number in the world and speak to any English-speaking person who answers using the same equipment and line.

When we work with our horse, the rein operates just like the handpiece on the phone. The horse's mouth acts like a switchboard operator. As long as you know the language the operator speaks, you can ask for any "business."

Once connected with the business you want, you make a request. When they agree to do what you ask, you hang up. So, too, you can pick up the rein and, assuming you know the language, speak with any part of the horse's body, make your request, then hang up when business is done.

We don't need one phone to talk to the horse's mouth, and another to his left hip, and another to his right shoulder, another to control the elevation of his head, and one to bend his body. Yet, that's what folks depend on — their seat, left leg here, right leg there, inside hand in one position, outside hand in another. That would be like using a different phone to call each workman. No wonder learning to ride can be so difficult.

HORSES RECOGNIZE PATTERNS MUCH QUICKER THAN PEOPLE DO. SO, EVEN IF YOU DON'T KNOW WHAT YOU ARE DOING, IF YOU ARE CONSISTENT, YOUR HORSE WILL GIVE YOU A CONSISTENT RESPONSE.

The right language

Can you imagine how complicated life would be if the plumber spoke one language, the cabinet maker another, the floor guy a third, the wallpaper hanger a fourth, and so on? Well, our horse has lots of employees or contractors, as it were — parts of his body that do different jobs — but, fortunately, they all speak the same language. So, not only can we use the same equipment to talk with any part of the horse's body, we can use the same language. It's getting easier for us and the horse.

In conversation, when we nod our head, it's assumed that we are saying "yes." We hear the term "lite," and we know that's code language for "lower in calories than the regular version." When we're driving, we use our directional signal, and that tells the other drivers, "We're planning to make a left-hand turn." **So communication, even at its most basic, involves learning lingo.**

The Helen Keller connection

The horse isn't born knowing rein language, so we'll have to teach it to him. Do you remember watching the story of Helen Keller? No one could get through to her — it seemed there was no effective means of communication — until one day at the well. She made the mental connection between the teacher's hand motions and "water." She realized that there was meaning to the movements. Once she understood "water," learning other words was easy.

Just as "water" was the foundation word for Helen Keller's language, "giving to the bit" is the foundation for the entire language we use in riding. When we teach our horse to give to the bit, we teach him one concept: We want a response from one part of his body when we take slack out of the rein. **When he gives the right response, we drop the rein, releasing him from the request.** Once he recognizes a pattern, he starts looking for other connections.

But, doesn't the horse get confused if you use the same rein to say lots of things? Sure he does at first, just as a person learning a language may have a hard time with new words. Confusion is a normal part of learning. But, it is short-lived if the rider is consistent.

So, when we pick up the rein thinking about the horse's hip, then release it when he moves the hip, he learns to recognize that pattern is related to the hip. When we then pick up the rein thinking about the left shoulder, he learns our left-shoulder-thinking pattern. If we try to get too complicated — using obvious body clues — we don't

This rider is talking to the horse's mouth via a telephone. When the horse does what she wants, she'll hang up. The rein acts the same way.

do as well, because we really can't be as consistent about obvious body cues as we are when we just think about what response we want. Those subtle changes in position or weight — sometimes too subtle for us to even recognize — are enough for the horse.

So, how does the horse know what part we're calling? We really don't know for sure. But, **when we think about one thing, we are different to the horse than when we think about something else.** Horses recognize patterns much quicker than people do; so, even if you don't know what you are doing, if you are consistent, your horse will give you a consistent response.

What really counts

So, the first part of being able to communicate with our horse is, essentially, recognition. The horse has to recognize our request, and, in order to be motivated to respond to it, it has to be important to him. Just as we recognize something as familiar when we see it a number of times, it becomes familiar to the horse when we repeat a request. But, how do we tell him it's important? After all, for a lot of horses, getting their rein pulled on is familiar, but they don't treat the signal as needing immediate attention.

Thinking logically, what do you recognize as important? Generally, important stuff falls into one of two categories — things that reward us and things that prevent us from experiencing pain of some sort. Going to work is important because we get paid in some form. And, we know brakes on our vehicle are important because they prevent us from having a wreck. So, too, getting paid and avoiding discomfort are high on your horse's priority list.

First things first. **Once we've taken the slack out of his rein, what the horse wants most in the whole world is for us to let go of his rein. So we make a deal with him.** If he does what we ask, we release the rein. He goes to work, we pay him. The more paydays he has, the more eager he is to come to work.

And, we all know horses are comfort-loving creatures, so avoiding discomfort is important. You can only prevent what you sense may be coming. There's no value putting your brakes on at random, hoping to avoid an accident. You brake when you sense something about to happen. The more warning you have, the better you can respond to the threat. That's what happens with our horse, too. **The slower we move our hands, the more time he has to recognize that we are about to take the slack out of his rein, and the quicker he moves to prevent the discomfort of the rein being adjusted.**

When we call the plumber, he gives us part of his day, his talent and his work in exchange for a paycheck. So, too, because he's learned that recognizing our signals is important to him, the horse turns over to us control of part of his body — the part we are calling on the phone. And so, he gives to the bit, spins left or picks up a right lead, depending on what body parts we talked to and what we asked them to do.

We must develop the language, so the horse can recognize it, respond to it, and turn control over to us.

In developing the language, we are going to have to answer four questions each time we want to tell the horse to do something.

1) What part of the horse's body do we want to talk to?

In the initial giving to the bit lessons we'll be talking to the horse's mouth. But, as we'll see in later chapters, we'll talk to various parts of his body — the muscles in his neck, his shoulders, front feet, barrel, and hind feet through the rein.

2) In what direction do we want it to move?

One factor in the new "language" is that every time we pick up the rein or lead rope, we expect our horse to move a part of his body.

3) What is the motivator? What will cause him to change from what he's currently doing to do what we want of him?

In almost all cases, it's our picking up the rein — the threat of the slack being taken out of the rein.

4) How will the horse know he moved the right part of his body in the direction we desired?

In almost all cases, it's the release of the rein.

With those four criteria in mind, we'll begin the process of teaching our horse to give to the bit. ■

7

So, What Is A Give?

When we ask our horse a question, we don't want a "no" or "maybe." We want a resounding "yes!" That "yes" is the same as "give."

When we ask our horse a question, there are three ways he can answer us — "give," "neutral" or "pull." If I asked you if you wanted something, you could answer with a "yes," "no" or "maybe." If I asked you if you wanted my new truck, your enthusiastic "yes" would be considered a "give." If, perchance, you hemmed and hawed and said, "maybe" (perhaps thinking I would sweeten the deal by throwing in the trailer — fat chance), I would consider that response as "neutral." And, if you walked away in disgust, I'd call that a "pull."

Have you ever seen a dog who wants a part of your hamburger? He first comes nosing around, then sits ever so nicely. Next he raises one paw. When that doesn't get the desired response, he switches paws or gives a little bark. Eventually, he sits up on his hindquarters and begs. When he does what we think is the cutest movement, we give him a piece of hamburger.

If our objective was to get him to put his right paw on our knee, we would say he "gave" with his paw when it was on our knee. When he walked away, he would be "pulling." When he sat there looking at us, he'd be in "neutral."

The horse does basically the same thing. He wants the release of the rein even more than the dog wants the meat. So the horse tries different options. By our timing the release to the performance we want, to when he "gives," moving the correct part of his body in the direction we want, he gets rewarded for the activity.

John uses what appears to us as the same cue to ask for Seattle's left front foot (top photo) to step left and his left hind foot to step left (bottom photo). How does Seattle know what John wants? In both cases, John uses the same rein cue and no conscious body/leg cues, but because John is thinking about one or the other of Seattle's legs responding, John himself is different from one cue to the next. With repetition, Seattle recognizes those subtle differences and knows what John wants.

Any part can give

The neat thing about the "giving to the bit" concept is that any part of the horse's body can give to the bit. When we begin, we ask the jaw to give. With the dog, we could have rewarded him when he put his paw on our knee, or we could have rewarded him when he wagged his tail. With repetition, he knows that when he does a certain thing, we'll give him a piece of our hamburger.

Because the rein is physically connected to the bit in the horse's mouth, we tend to think we are talking to the mouth when we pick up the rein. But, let's think of it another way. Let's pretend that the rein splits into about 20 other lines when it reaches the bit — like the phone line out of our house connects with millions of other lines at the switching station. We use the same rein to talk with any part of the horse's body. So, if we want the horse's hips to move over, we take all the slack out of the rein and wait for him to move his hips.

Initially, the horse may give his jaw to the bit, but when we continue to hold the rein, the horse continues to give back through his body until the hips start to move. When we get the response we desire, we release the rein. Giving from the jaw all the way through the horse's body to the hip takes lots of practice.

Any part can pull

When we call a part of the horse's body, he has the option of giving, being in neutral or pulling. If we are asking the right front foot to step to the right, for instance, and instead he moves it to the left, that would represent a "pull." If he moved it forward or back, but neither left or right, that would be like "neutral," and if he moved it slightly back and to the left, that would be a slight pull. **These distinctions may seem obvious, but when you are holding a rein and wondering if you should release it or not, they become important.**

The natural tendency of a person or a horse is to pull when pulled on. If the horse pulls on the rein, the rider's natural response is to match tension for tension. But that only keeps things at a status quo; neither side is "giving." In the "giving to the bit" exercises, we are going to have to train ourselves;

a) not to pull on the rein, but to just take the slack out of the rein,

b) to differentiate between a pull, neutral and a give,

c) to wait for the horse to give,

d) to release the rein entirely, the moment the horse gives.

So, how do you begin

In order to build our language, we have to have a beginning word. That beginning word is "give your jaw to the side." So, when we ask for a give and our horse ignores our request, or worse yet, pulls on the rein, he's telling us he doesn't understand our word or, if he does have the gist of what we want, he isn't conditioned to respond to it. If I said, "There's a snake" to someone who didn't understand English, I wouldn't necessarily get any reaction from them. But, if I said the same thing to someone who understood what I meant, they'd quickly ask "Where?" or move to what they knew to be a safe spot. They wouldn't have to stop to think about responding or not.

That's where we begin with our horse — developing an initial word that he responds to without having to think before responding. That will do two things: It will get him in the habit of responding to our request, and it will give us one word from which we can build a language. Incidentally, the particular word we chose to start with has great benefits in terms of the horse's performance, allowing the horse to give us athletic responses.

All of Zip's performance training is based on the "giving to the bit" lesson, from the precise placement of his feet to collection.

First we are going to develop the "baby give," the give to the side with the horse's jaw. We'll use this as a building block for the rest of the training. If you want excellent control of your horse, and plan to do any type of sophisticated work, such as showing, working cattle, dressage and so forth, then you'll want to teach your horse to "give to the bit," asking the horse to "give" with his jawbone. **Once he gives with his jaw, then we'll ask him to go through specific giving exercises, relaxing various muscles in his neck, withers and back.** This is the technique that lets you ask the horse for collection, or to elevate his shoulders so he can step off into the lope nicely. This process of teaching the horse to give to the bit is systematic and requires thousands of repetitions, but the payoff is tremendous.

Once the horse learns to give all the way through his body, then we'll "connect" the rein to the feet; that is, we'll use the giving language to talk with every part of the horse's body. We'll be able to position him anyway we like, just using the rein and release of the rein. So if you'd like a beautiful strike-off into the lope, not only will you have the horse's body soft, but you can easily position him to step off into either lead or to change leads smoothly.

The hand movements

With the horse standing still and wearing a snaffle bit bridle, preferably a full cheek snaffle, let both reins just hang on the horse's neck so they are even. You'll want your reins connected, preferably with a smooth connection, like on a very long roping-style rein, not like split reins. I usually work with a smooth rein about ten feet long from one side of the bit to the other.

We are going to work with the left side of the jawbone first. Your left hand will talk to the spot on your horse's jaw; your right hand will help your left hand. As you start working through this exercise, you'll find that you can set up a rhythm that makes the whole exercise go smoother than making movements at random.

Step #1 — Pick up the center of the rein with your right hand, that is, where the buckle would be on English reins, or where the rein lays on the horse's mane when it droops evenly on both sides. This is the set-up step. Raise your right hand about 12 inches.

Step #2 — Reach part way down the left rein with your left hand. (Don't lean forward while you do this. Don't move your left shoulder forward.) Grasp the rein firmly and close your hand into a

Left, letting the rein droop on both sides of the horse's neck, the rider reaches down to the center of the rein. She lifts the rein with her right hand (step #1).

Below, the rider stretches her arm forward to grasp the left rein with her left hand (first part of step #2).

Right, the rider braces her rein hand against the swell of the saddle (second part of step #2).

Below, the rider has totally released the rein (step #7). She will count two seconds, and then pick up the rein again with her right hand to ask for another give (step #1).

death grip on the rein. Bring your left hand back toward you so you can brace it against the pommel or swell of the saddle. Lock it into position.

While you are bringing your hand back to the saddle, if you run into resistance — that is, if you'd have to pull on the horse's mouth in order for your hand to reach the saddle — then let go of the rein (before you do pull) and reach for it again, this time with more rein between the horse's nose and where you reach. **Your goal is to pick up the rein at a distance where you can bring your hand back to the saddle, putting contact or only very slight tension into the rein, not enough that you are pulling on the horse. If you have moved your horse's jaw one-eighth of an inch, you have pulled on him.**

If you have moved your hand to the saddle and there is still slack in the rein, it's the job of the right hand to pull the rein through your left hand until the slack is gone.

Step #3 — When you have the correct amount of contact with the left rein, open your right hand and let the excess rein fall out. Drop your right hand down near the saddle; don't keep it up in the air.

Step #4 — Wait.

Step #5 — Wait.

Step #6 — Wait.

Step #7 — When the horse moves his jawbone energetically to the left, open the fingers of your left hand and let the rein drop out, giving the horse lots of slack. That is what we call the "release."

The release is like a paycheck. If you are stingy with your horse's pay, he'll be stingy with his work. If you are generous with your release, then he'll be generous with his give. Be sure that when you release the rein, you let it go totally. Then start the process again.

Begin again by picking up the middle of the rein with your right hand. Getting the mechanics down is the easy part; developing the feel is not so easy. But once you have it, you can solve nearly any problem that your horse will present to you.

Pulling against a post

You have to brace your hand. It is not optional. Even after doing this for 20 years, I still brace my hand because I know it will help the horse learn faster than if he can move my hand. In most three-day clinics, there are riders with a broad range of experience. The most experienced riders often do not brace their hand against the saddle, acting either out of habit or the belief that their experienced feel will be able to release on time. Those with the least riding ability often do exactly as they are told and get better results. During the course of the three days, riders of all experience levels find their hand down by their knee or out to the side, or behind their leg, or who knows where when it isn't braced against the saddle. **Those riders who brace their hand against the saddle get the best results.**

This is because the more immovable the object that the horse pulls against, the more he believes he cannot move it and the quicker he stops pulling. If I tied a feather to a horse and asked him to trot off, he'd have no problem. But, if I tied a tractor to him, he wouldn't get very far, and pretty soon he'd quit trying. When the horse learns he can't pull on the bit and get the reins released, he'll explore other options, which is what we want him to do.

Dumb and dumber

In the photos that follow, we'll pretend that I am the horse and the telephone post is the rider's hand. The rope between us is the rein. I can jerk on that post all day long, and the post won't be impressed by my strength. The post won't care. It won't budge. It doesn't matter if I exert a steady pull or a quick jerk. (The only jerk in that scenario would be me.)

Now, let's say that one time when I was pulling, the post moved one quarter of an inch. Say that I pulled 20 times, and on the 20th time it moved a smidge. That would encourage me to keep pulling. Let's say I now pull another 23 times, and on the 23rd time, the post moves. What would I have learned? I've learned that I need to keep pulling, because eventually it will give.

That's what happens with the horse. He will pull against your hand. If your hand is braced and immovable 19 times but he can get you to budge the 20th, you've taught him to pull. That's why consistency is so important. (The moral to this story is that you have to be dumber than a post to train a horse.)

The release

The release is what the horse waits for, once he knows the arrangement. So, knowing when to release, to pay the horse, is important. **If you determine that the horse isn't pulling and he isn't in neutral, but he has moved his jawbone energetically to the side (where you are holding the rein), then you should release the rein entirely — immediately.**

John, pretending to be the the horse, is jerking on the post, which represents the rider's fixed, immovable hand.

A pull can come from any direction. Here John is pulling down on the post. That still represents a pull, and not a "give."

This is still a pull. If we release when the horse pulls lightly, we're still teaching him that it requires a pull of the reins for him to get a release.

John is in "neutral" in this photo (above). There is slack in the rein, but he isn't pulling, nor is he "giving" to the post.

Below, John "gave" to the post. He moved his hand energetically toward the post. Obviously, the post never moved.

While this seems relatively straightforward, it requires tremendous concentration to put into practice. Participants in my clinics spend three full days learning what I'm teaching you here — and they have me and often some of my associates there to help them. Before each student even gets on their horse, we practice with a rein. I pretend to be the horse. As the rider, they brace their hand and I pull, go neutral, and give. We go through minutes of "That's a pull, that's a pull, that's a give, that's a pull, that's a neutral, that's a neutral, that's a pull, that's a give," so that they are not distracted by being on the horse and having to release on time.

While it takes years to develop really good hands, learning to release doesn't take long at all. The rule of thumb is: **Release if the horse isn't pulling or in neutral, because he's probably giving. If you think he's giving, you are probably right**.

Once you've decided, don't talk yourself out of it. If you've guessed wrong, you will sort that out over time. **It's the consistency of the release that lets the horse know he's done what you want.** Sometimes the horse will give, then pull before you can release. You can only release on the give, so you have to wait for another give or you'll be teaching your horse to give, then pull. Horses learn patterns quickly. So, if you make a mistake, it will be a random movement, not necessarily part of a pattern. However, consistent mistakes will lead to consistent behavior from the horse that you don't want. That's why we say that first comes the rider's concentration, then the rider's consistency, then the horse's performance.

Once you've practiced the hand movements off the horse, or with the horse standing still, ask him to walk. It's easier for the horse to learn to give to the bit at the walk than at any other gait or even stopped. Because you are going to use the rein to establish a giving arrangement with the horse's jawbone, you can't also use the rein to steer. So, ride in an enclosed area where you won't have to worry about where the horse goes. It won't matter if he's near the rail or out in the middle, as long as you stay safe; you are going to focus your concentration on just one thing.

Putting hand movements into practice

When you take all the slack out of the rein, your horse doesn't have a clue what you want. He just knows what he wants, and he wants you to let go of the rein. **The bit acts as a motivator; it causes the horse to change. It doesn't tell him what to change, but it motivates him to do something in order to get you to release the rein.**

The horse then starts on a treasure hunt to see what will get you to release the rein. If I told you I'd give you $100 if you can guess my middle name, you'd start calling out names. The only way you'd know that you guessed the right one was if I told you it was right and paid you the $100.

The horse doesn't know why there's tension on the rein, and he only knows that he wants you to let go of it. He may take the direct approach, pulling on your hand. Depending on his personality and previous experience, he may lean against the bit, thinking he'll drag the rein away from you. He may pull hard and fast, thinking he'll jerk the rein out of your hand. He may turn his head far to the right, actually turning himself in circles trying to stretch the rein out of your hand. He may just get frustrated and throw a tantrum, thinking he'll resolve the situation that way. He may just stand there doing nothing, for a long, long time, thinking that eventually you'll give up. He may use a combination of these tactics, which is why keeping your hand solidly braced against the saddle is so important.

Because the horse may have such varied responses, you have to be prepared to wait, but then to release when the give finally happens. The first give always takes the longest time.

The longest that I've ever had to wait for the first give was 45 minutes. But the next 99 gives only took a total of an hour and 15 minutes, the following 100 gives took 45 minutes, the next 100 took 18 minutes, the next 100 took 14 minutes, and the fifth 100 gives took only 10 minutes. In less than three hours, a horse who had never given to the bit before — who took 45 minutes to give once — gave 500 times. Most horses catch on much quicker. I'll warn you that the rider will be more tired — from concentrating — than the horse will, and while 500 gives may sound like a lot, it's really just a good beginning.

Getting into a rhythm helps. I hold until the horse gives, then I release immediately. I count two seconds, getting my hand movements into a rhythm, so that at the end of two seconds, I am asking for the next give.

Release quickly

The quicker you release when the horse gives you the right answer, the quicker the horse will get the message that he did what you wanted. If you think the horse has given, release immediately before he does something else, whether it be moving his feet or moving his jaw. The horse will give you the right answer before he actually knows it's the right answer, so he's likely to still be in treasure-hunt mode while you're figuring out whether to release or not.

"You have to be 'dumb' as a post to train a horse," says John.

That's because we try to make asking our horse to give too complicated — in fact, we make all of horse training more complicated than it has to be. In the post photos, the post matches John pound for pound, just by

holding its position. When John puts 50 pounds of pressure on the rope, the post naturally exerts 50 pounds of pressure on its end of the rope. If the post had 51 pounds, it would pull John toward itself. If John had 51 pounds, and the post only 50, he'd likely move the post.

Like the post, once we've taken slack out of the rein, we should hold our hand in a fixed position and wait for the horse to give. If we let our hand "float," we'll likely pull harder on the horse when he pulls on us, or we'll continue to pull as he gives, because it's natural to match pull for pull. ■PH■

8

Commonly Asked Questions

*Your goal is to control one part of the horse's body
at a time. But, getting there takes
patience, persistence and technique.*

We know that a horse (or a person, for that matter) must be motivated in order to change his behavior. It can happen one of two ways, either with a negative motivator — pain or the fear of something bad happening — or with a positive motivator, a reward or the expectation of something pleasurable. Experience tells us that horses can get used to negatives such as fear or pain. When that happens, a level of fear or pain that worked at one time is no longer motivational, because the horse has learned he can live through it. So, to get the same response, we'd have to raise the level of pain or fear — not a pretty picture. Eventually, using this system leads to a wreck.

A positive motivator is stronger than a negative one for anything beyond the short run. The horse learns to give to the bit — or to do any other behavior — because he feels a reward in doing it.

For example, the horse who holds onto a fence and cribs/sucks wind continues that behavior because it feels good. Once a horse gets "hooked," no amount of negative pressure — yelling at him, throwing rocks at him (we shudder), electric wires on the fence line and so forth — is likely to get him to stop cribbing. Positive feedback is more influential than negative consequences.

A horse may just happen to do a particular behavior the first time, whether it's cribbing or giving to the bit. But, he repeats it because he receives a reward. He then becomes confirmed in that behavior when the reward is consistent.

Learning to identify a "give" is important to knowing when to release. Here a helper points out the exact spot the rider should watch to see the horse give. It's a movement to the side, which is also slightly back toward the rider. You can teach the horse to give from in the saddle or from on the ground. And, the rider can learn to identify the "give" by sight or by feel.

The technique

So, our job as the rider is to set up a condition in which the horse can do what we want him to do consistently, so we can reward him consistently. To ask a horse to give to the bit, we take all the slack out of one rein (without pulling on the horse's mouth) and hold the rein steady. **When the horse moves his jaw energetically toward the tightened rein (even if it's only a quarter of an inch), we release the rein immediately, rewarding his movement.** With repetition, he learns that every time he "gives" us his jaw, we release the rein.

You know that once you've taken all the slack out of the rein, there are three options for the horse. He can pull against you — either up, down, to the "wrong" side or a combination of these movements. He can go into neutral where you feel that nothing is happening — as if there's no horse on the end of the rein. The last option, and usually the last one the horse tries, is moving his jaw to the side, toward your hand. This is the one you want. When this happens, you should let go of the rein so that the horse feels a total release, a lack of pressure from or contact with either rein.

Normally, after the rein is released, the horse will bring his head out in front of his body again. This is exactly what you want. You will be riding your horse with him looking forward, not with his head off to the side. We ask him to move his head to the side only as a technique, an exercise, to get him to relax his neck muscles. When a muscle is stiffened or tensed in the horse's neck, we cannot control it, and other muscles farther back in the horse's body stiffen up as well. When he bends his neck, he can move more athletically; that also gives us a way to develop control of other parts of the horse's body, like his feet, shoulders and hips.

Once you understand the "giving" procedures and then put them into practice, certain questions always seem to arise.

Q. *When I take up the slack in the rein asking for a baby give, won't that tell the horse to go in circles? Isn't that confusing to him?*

A. Initially, he'll probably walk in circles. Most horses do, but we're not concerned with where he's traveling (staying safe, though, of course). And, while he may initially think you want him to walk in circles, when you don't release the rein, he'll explore other options. Eventually he'll figure out that you are talking to his jawbone, not his feet. And, yes, it is confusing at first, but that only lasts a short time. Basically, you're teaching your horse a new language, and the first day of language study is always a little confusing. But, because you are using a specific signal and giving him a reward he really wants, even the first day of "giving" training is usually less confusing to the horse than was the old system of riding.

Q. *What do you do if the horse keeps walking in circles?*

A. Just keep asking for the baby give and allow him to continue walking the circles. One of the benefits of this lesson is that the horse learns to follow his nose and learns to make a correct circle. As we get him softer, working through the more advanced giving, then we can use the give to make the circle larger or smaller. If you feel the circles are getting too small, or you are getting dizzy, after a release, you can begin practicing with the other rein, which will probably make the horse turn circles the other way. As you vary the rein without pulling the rein too tight, the circles will probably open up.

Q. *When I try the "giving to the bit" exercises while on the trail, my horse turns off the path. Should I use leg pressure to try to steer him?*

A. No. Don't be concerned with steering at this point. It's easiest to teach this exercise in an enclosed area, like a round pen or arena. That way, you and the horse can stay safe, and you provide a classroom environment for the horse. That also allows you to focus just on teaching the give. It's really distracting to try to teach this lesson on the trail or with other horses working in the area.

Once the horse has the give down pat, you can do it anywhere. You would do better to fence off an area or to trailer your horse to somewhere with a fence for the first few days' practice than to distract yourself and confuse the horse by using leg pressure.

Q. *I understand that once I've asked the horse to give, I shouldn't release the rein until he gives. But, what if he starts going too fast, or I can't control him?*

A. Rules No. 1 and No. 2 of horse training take precedence over everything else all the time — you can't get hurt and your horse can't get hurt. If you feel unsafe, do whatever you have to do to have your horse under control — and if that means releasing the rein early, do it. You can always ask for the give again once the horse is under control, or work with him from the ground. In fact, working on the ground is a great way for both you and your horse to learn this lesson. Whatever you do, don't compromise your safety.

Q. *Whenever I take the slack out of the rein, my horse stops.*

A. That is one of the normal responses. Tell him to keep walking. If he doesn't walk when you ask, you'll have to teach the cue to go forward (the "speed up" cue).

To teach him to speed up, using both your legs, bump your horse's sides until he moves forward. Keep bumping until he gives you a noticeable change in leg speed, then stop bumping. You don't have to kick hard, just keep bumping until you get the response you want.

Q. *What does it look like when the horse "responds energetically"?*

A. It looks as if the side of the bit suddenly felt hot to the horse, so he moved his head to the side. It doesn't have to be a big movement. A good "baby give" can be an energetic movement of a quarter of an inch or as much as four inches. We're not concerned with the amount of movement, only that the horse moves his head in the direction we're asking.

Q. *What is the hardest part for people to understand?*

A. The importance of rider consistency is the hardest part to understand. Riders often concentrate when they are in the arena, teaching the horse that every time they touch the rein the horse should have a light, energetic response with his jawbone. But, then, as soon as they lead him out of the gate, they allow the horse to lean on the reins or they pull him with the lead rope. The horse doesn't know when your signals don't count.

Q. *When you interview students who've learned what giving to the bit is about, what was the biggest eye-opener for them?*

A. Most riders are used to influencing their horses mechanically, for instance, pulling on one rein to indicate the direction they want the horse to go. When riders figure out that the horse should move his own head or body, that the rein should not mechanically move the horse, then they learn they are setting up the conditions and waiting for the horse to respond.

Q. *What adjustments have these riders had to make in their riding?*

A. The most obvious is learning to focus and be consistent. That takes quite a while. Beyond that, usually riding with one rein is awkward at first, learning to speak to only one side of the horse's mouth at a time. For that, it's helpful to practice the hand movements off the horse. The idea of one hand feeding the rein to the other is strange to some riders. But some already know how to shorten their reins by having one hand pull the rein through the other hand, so they have a head start.

It's also difficult to stick with one rein when the horse feels like he's going out of control. The less in control the horse is, the more important using just one rein is. That takes getting used to.

Q. *After my horse gives and I release, he pulls his head down toward the ground. What should I do?*

A. You should shorten the time between requests, asking him to give, then give again. Don't speed up your hand movements, just ask again sooner. The ideal timing is that you release and count "one 1,000, two 1,000." On the word "one" your rein hand should close around the rein. By the word, "two" your rein hand should have

This rider is teaching the horse to give to the bit correctly. Note the rider's hand fixed against the saddle. In a correct baby give, the horse's head moves from out in front of him to the side.

brought the rein back to the saddle, and your other hand should be starting down toward the horse's withers.

On the last "thousand" your rein hand should be braced against the saddle. It's as if you've placed a phone call and the phone is ringing — you have to wait for the horse to answer your call. As you practice the hand movements, you'll be better able to set up a rhythm that will make it easier.

Q. *I normally ride in a curb bit or hackamore. Can I do the same training with them instead of a snaffle bit? Can I teach the horse to give to the bit with a halter?*

A. While you can apply some of the same concepts using a curb or hackamore, it's important to be able to speak to one side of the horse's mouth at a time, which you can't do using anything but a simple broken-mouth snaffle. In addition, those operate on a leverage principle, which is not compatible with what we are trying to do.

You could work with a halter, but it wouldn't send as clear a signal as the snaffle bit. However, once the horse has learned to give to the bit, we will expect him to give to the halter, whether we are leading him from the ground or riding him.

Q. *I'm teaching my horse to give to the bit because he gets out of control on the trail. How long will it take before I can go back on the trail?*

A. Generally, it only takes a few weeks of serious work, but no two horse-and-rider combinations take exactly the same length of time. Learning to focus and getting consistent as a rider takes the longest time, along with learning to recognize the moment when you first begin to lose control. Horses are usually out of control long before the rider recognizes it.

Q. *My horse bucks. I'm beginning to teach him to give to the bit, but what else should I do?*

A. If your horse has a bucking problem, he should be restarted as a green horse, not from the ground but from the saddle. In addition to giving to the bit, you'll want to do a series of instructional exercises, circles, stops, backing up, cone exercises, transitions, variations of speed, diagonal movement and so forth. That way you control his speed and transitions better — by asking him to do specific things you are solving a problem by replacing the problem with good performance. But, giving to the bit is where it all begins. It's the first thing I teach an unbroke horse when I mount him for the first time. Before he's even moved his feet, I start asking him to give to the bit. That's the day in his life that I'd have least control of him, and the most important thing to teach him is the give.

Q. *Does it ruin your training if you've been working on "giving to the bit" exercises in the arena, and then you go out on the trail and use two reins to stop the horse?*

A. No, it doesn't ruin the training. The ideal, of course, is to be consistent with your use of the rein, but safety is paramount. I suggest that people ride the horse in a snaffle bit in the arena at home, working on control exercises and teaching the horse to give to the bit. If they don't feel they have enough control with the snaffle bit to go out on the trail, they should put whatever bit in the horse's mouth that gives them control. Then, after the trail ride, they should work with the snaffle bit in a controlled environment and continue to do that until they feel safe taking the horse on the trail in their snaffle bit. You should realize, though that most people have less control than they think they have with a curb or hackamore. And, the snaffle is designed to change a horse's direction, so using two snaffle reins to stop the horse is generally less effective than using just one.

Q. *I've been working on asking my horse to give, and I'm counting the gives. We're up to 8,000. He gives more willingly on the right side than the left. Does it make sense to ask him more on the left?*

A. Yes, the horse is never equal in his response, no matter how far we go in his training. It's the rider's responsibility to determine which side is not working as well as the other and work it two, three or four times more than the good side. Eventually, the bad side will be better than the good side. Then you'll work more on the side that used to be the good side.

Q. *How would you describe the difference between giving to the bit and the technique of turning the horse's head left and right before you get on him?*

A. Giving to the bit doesn't have anything to do with getting the horse's head to the side, although the result is that he moves his head to the side. It has to do with the feel of the jawbone and getting the horse to respond to a request. You're referring to pulling the horse's head around. You can only go so far with that type of training;

This rider is doing the right thing. Her hand is braced against the saddle and she's waiting. The horse isn't thinking about giving. He's focused on pulling, but that will change with time.

you end up steering the horse as though he were a stick. When we ask the horse to give, we can get both basic control and softness or responsiveness — a higher performance level from the horse. It would be very difficult to do dressage or reining work with the other system.

Although teaching the horse to give to the bit is slower than steering him around, it allows a great deal more responsiveness from the horse's body, and therefore we can do more with it.

Q. *Sometimes it feels like the horse is out of gas. He goes into neutral, just leaning on the bit. Should I bump him in the ribs?*

A. Yes, ask him to move. That's one reason it's easier to ask for the give at the walk than stopped. As he moves along, he'll want to use his neck to balance his stride, so he's more likely to figure out how to get you to release the rein.

Q. *Once the horse is giving at the walk, do you speed up and work at the trot, then the lope?*

A. Yes. Practice the give in all the gaits and at various speeds. The give stays the same no matter how fast we go, although you'll find it more difficult to coordinate at the faster speeds. We want the horse to turn over control to us of individual parts of his body so we can guide him around the dance floor at any speed.

Are you still having problems?

■ *Is the rein you are using too short?*

The type of rein that John uses — a long roping rein — makes it easiest. The rein has enough weight that the horse easily feels any hold you put on it, and it drops down when you release.

If your rein is too short, the horse won't get enough release to be meaningful. Laced reins are particularly difficult to work with because they don't slide through your hands easily and don't slide down the horse's neck (during the release).

The ideal length of rein for most horses is 10 feet, about 5/8 of an inch thick.

Learning to be a consistent rider is the hardest part of this lesson. Despite having worked several hours focusing entirely on being consistent with the rein, as the mare reaches down suddenly to deal with a fly, the rider pulls on the rein. The alternative to pulling or letting the rein droop, risking the horse stepping on the rein, is for the rider to ask for another give.

■ *Are you looking for too much movement in the give or asking the horse to bend his head around too much?*

If your horse is going in very tight circles or losing his balance, you may be taking up too much slack in the rein. When you are first teaching the give, you want the starting place for the horse's head each time to be out in front of him, not to the side.

■ *Are you pulling on the horse?*

You'll want to make sure that you are not moving the horse's head the first few inches when you pick up the rein.

■ *Have you remembered to put the hand that is not asking for the give down by the horse's withers?*

If not, there will be tension/contact on the other side of the horse's mouth, and he won't be free to give.

■ *Are you generous?*

It's better to release if you think the horse might have given, than to hold out for a bigger movement. The more often you reward the small movements or even a correct thought, the more the horse will repeat them.

■ *Are you releasing the rein immediately and completely when you recognize that the horse is giving?*

If not, he'll be doing something else by the time you release, and he won't know what he did to get a reward.

■ *Do you pull on the horse's rein at times other than when you are asking for the give — as in leading him with the reins, when tacking him up, when changing directions or when talking with a friend?*

It's the same rein attached to the horse's bit, whether you are on the ground or on his back. If you pull inadvertently on his mouth as you close the arena gate or as you are mounting, and then release your pull randomly, you are sending confusing signals. ■PH

Notes

9

Asking For The "Baby Give"

You plant the seed, and you have to be patient.
Then you can enjoy the harvest.

You, as a rider, are like a corn farmer. The farmer buys a field, prepares and fertilizes the soil, plants the corn seed, then waits a few days. He then goes out into the field and uncovers the seed to see how it is doing. When he doesn't see anything, he covers it back up again and gives it more water. A few days later, he goes out into the field, uncovers the seed and starts pulling on it, and a green stem appears. He pulls until the green stem is just tall enough to stick up out of the soil, then covers the seed over again.

A few days later, he pulls on the stem until he's got a little green plant. Three weeks later, he thinks it's time for some leaves, so he gets his Super Glue and glues leaves on the plant. He's sure that corn on the cob is coming right away, so he goes inside to boil water. Right? Of course not.

Well, maybe it's like this: The farmer prepares the ground, plants the seed and waits. When he sees a little green thing sticking up, he gets so excited that he gets out a scrub brush and starts washing the stem. When he finally sees leaves, he puts all his energy into waxing and polishing the leaves, but doesn't water the seed. You say, "Oh, come on, John, if you just polish the leaves, the plant won't live past the leaf stage to grow corn. If you want corn, you have to take care of the seed, and just wait."

You are right. The farmer's responsibility is to take care of the seed. If he only takes care of the plant that is above the ground, the plant is going to die. As soon as the farmer quits taking care of the seed — even though he can't see it — the plant will die.

Teaching a horse to give to the bit properly is just like planting corn. You have to make all the right preparations, take care of the seed, then just wait. If you work on the part that seems to be making progress, ignoring the seed, the horse's performance will die. If you just teach a horse to "break at the poll" or "set his head," it's like polishing the leaves; the horse's "give," or ability to respond to the rein in a meaningful way, like the corn plant, will not develop.

The control seed

You, the rider, will plant a control seed in the jawbone of the horse. If you put your finger through the ring of the snaffle bit onto the horse's lower jaw, you'll touch the spot that I refer to as the jawbone. In clinics I put a mark on that spot so riders know exactly what we are talking about. That spot, or seed, is about the size of a quarter. By controlling that spot, we can control the whole horse.

You might remember an illustration that I use about a coin. Pretend you are walking down a sidewalk and see a coin. You recognize it has value and so are motivated to bend down and pick it up. For one moment, your fingers are "controlled," as it were, by the coin, when you bend to pick it up. Of course, that means for that moment the coin also controls your thoughts and your body; it stops your feet and makes you lower your head as you bend down. That's the same principle we will use in teaching the horse to give to the bit. We're going to use a spot the size of a quarter to control the whole horse. We're going to get that spot to recognize us, respond to our request and turn over control.

No one would disagree that if I could get the spot on your horse's jawbone to cross a creek, your whole horse would cross the creek. Or, if I could tell the spot to get into the trailer up by the feed manger, the whole horse would be in the trailer. **So, instead of trying to tell all 1,000 pounds of horse to get into a trailer or to respond to us under saddle, we're going to tell one little spot, and let that spot control the whole horse.**

Back to the cornfield

Part of taking care of the corn seed is keeping rocks and weeds out of the cornfield. Once the farmer removes a rock from the field, he

John is using a livestock paint stick to mark giving spots on Seattle: the #1 Spot (above), the #2 Spot (below).

never has to take that same rock out of the field again. He can go to town for three or four months and know those same rocks won't be in his field. But, the field may be overgrown with weeds.

Like the farmer taking care of the seed, you'll have to take care of the "control seed" on your horse. When you get all the rocks and weeds away from that seed and take care of the seed, you'll see results.

Once you've taken all the slack out of the rein, asking the horse to give to the bit, what the horse wants most in life is for you to let go of the rein. Because that's what he wants, he's motivated to see what he can do to get you to let go. But, the obvious thing he'll do is pull against you. A solid pull against your hand is like a rock in the field; it will prevent the corn from growing. The horse can pull down, or forward, or down and around. He can pull toward one knee or pull up. He can lean against your hand, or do nothing, then try to jerk the rein from your hand. What you must do is lock your hand against the saddle and don't let it move. When the horse doesn't get a release by pulling, he tries other options, including giving.

Another option the horse can try is to go into neutral. This is when he doesn't pull, but neither does he give. Neutral is like having weeds in the field — it interferes with crop growth. Don't release on neutral, either, or you'll be encouraging the growth of weeds.

The third option is that the horse will give, or move that spot on his jawbone, with energy, in the direction of the rein. If he just barely puts slack into the rein, he is only "pulling less" or going into neutral, but not giving. **A give happens with energy, like the horse discovered that the bit was hot if he pulled on it.**

At the moment when the horse gives, you should totally release the rein, telling him that he did what you wanted. The more often the horse gives and you release the rein, the quicker he'll learn the lesson and the crop (his performance) will grow.

The first few gives

Now, the hard part is the first few times, when you lock your rein hand against the saddle and wait. The first give takes the longest. The horse doesn't know what you want from him, so he has to experiment. When he finally guesses the right move (the give) and you release the rein, rewarding him, then he has a clue what you

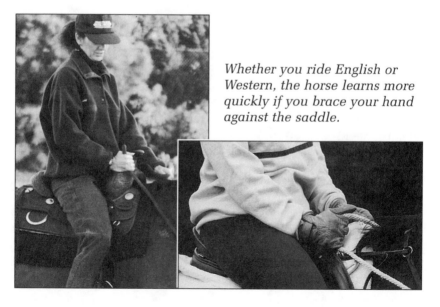

Whether you ride English or Western, the horse learns more quickly if you brace your hand against the saddle.

want, but not the whole picture. For all he knows, you released the rein because he swished his tail. He might have been thinking about his tail while he inadvertently moved his jawbone. The next time you take the slack out of the rein, he may swish his tail, expecting you to release the rein, and be confused because you don't release. Then he's back at square one trying to figure out what you want.

When he gives and you release, we'll count that as "one" when we begin counting. You are going to ask again, within two seconds, so that you can practice asking the horse to give thousands of times.

Repetition, repetition, repetition

As with every lesson, we want to train the physical, mental and emotional parts of our horse. Your horse will physically do what you are asking him long before he mentally understands your cue. Initially, it will be a random movement, then a random movement that gets repeated often enough that he recognizes a pattern. The rider has to resist the temptation to assume that when the pattern begins to form, the horse understands what the rider wants.

Once the horse is physically doing what the rider wants, and recognizing a rider's movement as a cue to him, then it's time for the emotional part of the training. Adding excitement, perhaps in the form of speeding the horse up or bringing another rider into the arena, will cause the horse's heart rate to go up. When that happens, his performance level will drop, and it will take an additional number of repetitions to get the same performance as before the excitement. **Nonetheless, because we are going to want our horse to respond to us in exciting situations, like on a trail ride or when a dog runs at him, we have to practice each lesson in a calm, then increasingly exciting environment.**

In addition, the horse will go through learning cycles — one time seeming to know the right answer, then seeming not to know. It's easy for the rider to become discouraged, to change the cue or to think that the horse is deliberately not cooperating.

One part at a time

We're going to develop control of the horse's body, one part at a time. I use nine "giving" spots between the jawbone and the withers to describe "giving to the bit" entirely through the horse. If you want lighter responses from your horses, better diagonal movements, better stops with the horse's front end light, better collection, better turns, smoother lead changes and elevation from the horse's withers so he can step higher or take longer strides, then you'll want all nine spots cooperating.

Whenever a horse locks up a part of his body, he stiffens a muscle group and tells you, "No, you can't have control of that part." He's also telling you that you can't have control of any part of his body farther back than that part. So, if the horse locks up his jaw, he's not going to respond to the rein at all. That's what happens when the horse suddenly bolts for home and you can't stop him. When he locks up his neck, you can't get a nice turn, and you'll also find that his back is stiff. When he locks up his shoulders, his feet become very heavy, and you can't get him to take the correct lead. When he locks up at the poll, he gets bouncy and uncomfortable to ride. Whenever you have trouble with one part of the horse's body not cooperating, check to see that the parts in front of that part are giving. If the corn leaves aren't looking too good, you can be sure there's a problem at below-ground level.

The money window

In this chapter and the next we will identify the nine positions or spots in which the horse can either lock up or pay up, like a bank teller who either refuses to give us any money or gives us all the money we ask for. When you're at the bank, the teller hands you money through a window. Well, the horse's performance pays off through the "money window" also. We say that we're at the money window when the horse's head is out in front of his body, not off to one side. But, we know that while top performance is there, so too is the most resistance. Remember that the performance we ultimately want from our horse happens with his nose out in front of him.

Don't ignore the money window. **It's not uncommon to get Spots #2 through #9, but if the horse doesn't give Spot #1 — starting from when his nose is lined up in front of his skeleton — his performance will still be stiff.** And, if you pull your horse's head off to the side, you'll never get performance when he's facing straight ahead. Spots #2 through #9 are of no real value without Spot #1, even though you may think the horse is soft to your rein once his head is off to the side. You only get paid real money through the money window.

But you might say, "Wait, John! If we get the horse's performance through the money window straight ahead, why are we asking the horse's nose to go to the side?" We do that as an exercise. When the

Teaching the spots is a training exercise. We don't ride our horses with their heads to the side; we ride facing ahead, through the "money window."

horse's nose is lined up to his skeleton directly, he can resist you with his whole frame. When we ask him to offset his nose, then he can't use his whole frame to resist our rein request. And, because getting the horse's head off dead-center is the difficult part, we have to be patient and wait for the horse to move his own head, rather than our dragging it around by the bit and rein. **Getting Spot #1 consistently is the hardest part of the entire "giving to the bit" process.**

Going through the spots is also a way of retraining the horse's muscles. We will systematically unlock each muscle group on both sides of the horse's neck, so that when he has his nose straight ahead, his neck still remains supple and he can respond to our requests fluidly, but we won't sacrifice Spot #1 in the process.

Spot #1

Each of the spots, in addition to being a location on the horse's body, is really a description of what happens at that location. Spot #1 is a spot about the size of a quarter on the horse's chin, one on each side of his mouth (see photo). In practice, it is the basic "baby give." Spot #1 occurs when the horse moves his head from facing straight ahead to the side where the rein is shortened. It takes lots of repetitions before you can confidently say that the horse has Spot #1 down pat — in fact about 2,500 repetitions. You'll do these by asking for 100 on one side, then switching to 100 on the other side, each time allowing the horse to bring his head to face forward again.

Many people make the mistake of pulling the horse's head off to the side, then asking for the give. That teaches the horse that when

You do not have to be riding to teach the horse to give to the bit. In these photos, John demonstrates hand positions if you are working from the ground. Ideally, the horse should be walking as you do this exercise. (Above) John picks up the rein with his right hand. (Below) John reaches for the rein with his left hand, holding the rein up with his right hand. He'll fix his left hand against the saddle, drop the rein with his right hand and wait for the horse to give — move his jawbone with energy toward John's left hand. When he does, we'll say that Spot #1 "gave."

The horse's head is in the Spot #2 position, and John is preparing to ask for another "baby give."

his head is off to the side and he's asked for a give, he should give more. But, since we don't want to ride him with his head to the side, and since getting the head from straight ahead to the side is really the hardest part of the give, that's where we begin. So Spot #1 teaches the horse to give to the rein by moving his jawbone from the facing-ahead position to the neck-bent position.

Spot #2

After hundreds of Spot #1 gives, you'll notice that the horse will leave his jawbone slightly off to one side instead of taking it back out front again. When you see that spot stay four inches off to one side, you will be working with the #2 Spot, which is just behind the horse's ears.

To illustrate how Spot #2 works, let's pretend I asked you to get me a drink of water. You hand me the water; I drink it and hand you the glass back. You wash the glass, dry it and put it away. Two seconds later, I ask you for another glass of water. You give it to me, I drink it and hand it back to you. Again you wash the glass, dry it and put it away. The third time I ask for water, you'll find yourself saying, "John, I'm just going to leave this glass on the counter, so it's handy for you next time." That's Spot #2. **Instead of the horse bringing his nose out in front of his body after he's given and you've released, he keeps it off to the side, so he's ready for your next request. The horse puts his own head into Spot #2 as a result of his responding to the giving request.** By him doing that, you'll know he's relaxed certain muscles of his neck.

In this process of "giving to the bit," we are going to systematically ask the horse to turn over control of his entire body, but just by asking the horse one easy question at a time, one that he can answer with a "yes." You're going to ask him to give, then give, then give, then give — each time just a "baby give."

Did I mention that it takes 3,000 repetitions to break a habit, and 15,000 more repetitions to replace that habit with a new habit? At a rate of asking the horse to give every two seconds, that takes.....well, lots of riding time at the walk, practicing the give to replace the old pulling-on-the-reins habit, with a please and thank you on your part and a give from your horse.

Just one thing: Just like the farmer taking care of the seed, you'll take care of the "baby give." And before long, both you and your horse will be enjoying the harvest. **PH**

10

Giving Spots #3 through #9

*You've planted the "corn seed," and if you care for it
through to Spot #9, you'll have a wonderful crop —
a horse on his way to upper-level performance.*

Suppose that you want your horse to stop moving his feet. You use your rein to communicate that request. He isn't going to stop because you pulled on the rein — he's going to stop because he knows that if he stops, you'll release the rein. **The rein isn't a mechanical brake stopping the horse. It's the promise of a paycheck if he does a good job.** That's the reason bits don't train horses. It doesn't matter what variety of pain you cause the horse by a severe bit; it's the release of the rein that the horse will work for. Consequently, we use the mildest bit that we can — the full cheek snaffle — and are prepared to release the rein immediately when the horse has done what we've requested.

When we use the rein to communicate with our horse, it's like sending signals electronically — like sending a fax — and waiting for a response. Both parties can't fax at the same time. Thus, we send our request and wait. The horse responds by moving his head, and we release the rein.

We started our "giving to the bit" lessons by asking one part of the horse — one little spot the size of a quarter on one side of his jawbone — to answer a request that we made through our rein. We took all the slack out of one rein, braced our hand against the saddle (as if we were a post) and waited for the horse to energetically move that spot toward our hand. When he did, we totally released that rein. **We call both that one spot and the movement the horse makes with it (the baby give) "Spot #1."**

Rein-handling sequence

Above left, John's right hand lifts the rein. His left hand reaches down to take all the slack out of the rein. Note that he does not move his shoulder forward as he reaches for the rein.

Above right, John fixes his left hand against the saddle and waits for Zip to give. It doesn't matter that Zip has stopped walking. John is only focused on waiting for the give.

Left, when the horse gives, John lets go of the rein and counts two seconds before asking for the give again. Note that Zip's head is waiting for John's next request — Spot #2.

In two seconds (literally) we asked the horse to give again: release, *1,000 one, 1,000 two,* pick up the rein, bring it back to saddle and hold. **After hundreds of Spot #1 responses, we found our horse in Spot #2.** (Using a livestock paint marker, we put a spot at the top of the horse's mane so we can see when the horse is in the Spot #2 position from the saddle.) **Spot #2 automatically happens when the horse leaves his head about four inches to the side for at least two seconds after we release the rein.**

In fact, each of the spots happens automatically as you continue to ask the horse to give. While you are working on Spot #1, #2 is beginning to happen. While you are working on #2, #3 is beginning to happen and so forth. That's part of the beauty of this system. If I asked you to do something that you were already almost doing, your answer would be "Sure, that's easy." By the time we are ready to ask our horse to consistently do Spot #3, for instance, he's already been doing it over 50 percent of the time. So, other than Spot #1, we're not teaching the horse anything difficult or foreign.

Practice, practice, practice

Practice in two-second intervals and in sets of 100 gives. Counting the gives is an extremely important part of this exercise. It gives you a goal — and a stopping place. It keeps you focused; you're less likely to become bored — or to give up because you're not sure if you are making progress. Counting also gives you lots of knowledge. You'll begin to see certain patterns or cycles: almost all horses do the same things at the same part of the cycle.

At the outset, counting "gives" may seem inconvenient or too much work. But, you can't expect your horse to improve if you don't do your full job, and that includes counting. Just to encourage you along, I'll tell you that Spots #1, #2 and #3 take the longest. In fact, when you look at the entire Spot #1 through #9 process, teaching Spot #1 takes about 50 percent of that time. The rest come amazingly fast if you've done the repetitions. It **might take you all day to get Spots #1 through #5, but then only 20 minutes to get from #6 to #9. But, we'll warn you, #1 through #3 may seem to take forever.**

Plan to count 100 gives on the left side, then 100 on the right. During the course of each 100, it's best not to take any breaks. Just allow the horse to continue walking, and practice the give at two-second intervals. Continue working through sets of 100, and you'll see the various spots we've spoken about just happen on their own.

And, don't be surprised that when you begin on the right, the horse seems not to have any idea what you want. That's because we have to condition each side of the horse to respond. So, you'll always have one side that is better than the other. But it won't be the same side. The bad side will become the good side.

As you work through the giving exercises, you'll be controlling specific muscle groups of the horse, and eventually the whole horse. Spots #1 through #4 are loosening-up or relaxing exercises. The result of the horse's relaxing the underside of his neck will be that he carries his neck correctly, becoming more beautiful.

As you read through the spots, you may find yourself confused. That's because these exercises are hard to visualize. Spots #6 through #9 may seem obscure, but that shouldn't stop you from trying to teach them to your horse. If all you understand is the baby give (Spot #1), just keep working with it. After a while, you'll see the others happen. By the time you are ready for Spot #6, it won't seem so foreign.

Mini-releases

As you proceed through the spots, you'll need to employ the mini-release. The full release — the dropping of the rein — tells the horse that he did what you asked of him, but the mini-release tells him he's on the right track; however, there's something more you want. So, for instance, if you want more than a Spot #1 give, then when the horse gives, you'll release the rein a little bit, but not so much that he can bring his head out in front of him again.

At that point, he may pull, go to neutral or give. Again, you wait for the give, then release or mini-release, depending on what your request was. After a while, when you give a mini-release, the horse will know he did some of what you wanted, and he'll in effect ask you what else he can do for you. Any time the horse gives, we should acknowledge the give, even if we don't fully release the rein.

Spot #3

Spot #3 is really a line, rather than a spot, although remember we're talking about performance that happens at particular locations on the horse's body. It's the line along the major muscle in the horse's neck. Spot #3 — the relaxation of the big muscle in the horse's neck — automatically happens as we continue to ask the horse for a "baby give" while he is in Spot #2, exactly as Spot #2 happened while we worked with Spot #1.

There are three things we'll be looking for from Spot #3, and they always happen in the same order. **We'll gradually see the Spot #3 line become parallel to the ground.** That means the lower neck muscle that has been doing all the work of holding the horse's head up is beginning to relax.

The muscle below the spot will begin to bounce, like Jello. It doesn't bounce up and down, but wobbles back and forth, indicating that the neck muscle is relaxing even more. You can't get supple performance from the horse if the major neck muscle is stiff.

Third, **we'll see the Spot #3 line take the shape of a pretty curve** — to the left if you are working on the left side, to the right if you are working on the right. That designates a further softening or relaxing of the neck muscles. **When Spot #3 happens, you are beginning to build an arc in your horse's body.** When you ride a horse in a circle, you'll eventually want his nose, his mane, his withers, his body and his tail all on the same circle, rather than his head and body operating like a truck and trailer. The Spot #3 arc is where that beautiful circle begins.

So, you'll know you have Spot #3 down pat when you have three things: the line parallel to the ground, the lower muscle wobbling and the pretty curve of the neck.

Sometimes horses put their heads in strange positions when they are trying to figure out what you want. At no time should the horse's head come farther to the side than John's right hand. If the horse's head does come, for example, as far back as your knee, raise your rein and forcibly push the horse's head forward.

Spot #4

Spot #4 is at the top of the horse's head, by his forelock. You can also clearly see Spot #3, the line down the big muscle of the horse's neck.

Spot #4 has to do with the elevation of the horse's head. Spot #4 — the forelock — can occur anywhere within eight inches of the elevation of the horse's withers. Now, the interesting thing about Spot #4 is that you can get an A, B or C grade with it, with A being the goal. **An A grade is when the forelock is four inches above the withers (that's easy to remember — forelock/four inches above).** If the forelock is even with the withers, you score a B. And C is when the line is four inches below the horse's withers.

Frequently, when you start the giving exercises, the horse's head is up too high. As he learns to give (Spots #1 and #2), his head comes down. At Spot #3, the line is parallel to the ground, and the neck is getting more and more relaxed, which means his head is dropping lower. His neck muscle may become so relaxed that his nose hangs. You know it's too low, but what are you going to do about it? **You didn't pull it down, so you are not going to pull it back up. You are going to just keep asking the horse to give, and as you do, he'll begin to give up instead of down.** Like every good teacher, you want your student to get an A, so you just keep working on the "baby give," until the horse's head comes up to an A.

Spot #5

If you sit in the saddle and look down at your horse's neck, there are any number of shapes that you might ordinarily see the neck taking. Sometimes the neck is straight for a few inches, then bends to the left or right. Sometimes it's straight all the way to the ears, and sometimes it forms an S-shape, or some variation of the above. We want one pretty, shapely arc, with no turns or straightened places. **Any time you see a straight place, or an atypical curve, your horse has stiffened a muscle in his neck. Whenever a neck muscle is stiffened, performance suffers.** We're going to continue working with the "baby give" until we see a beautiful curve in his neck. **That beautiful curve from the withers to the poll (the top of the horse's head right between his ears) is Spot #5.**

At the same time Spot #5 happens, in addition to Spots #1 through #4, you may notice that your horse is beginning to walk in a relaxed, round circle — the same curve as you see on his neck. Just as with Spots #2, #3 and #4, keep asking Spot #1 for the "baby give" in series of 100 gives, and you'll find Spot #5 happening.

Relaxing vs. flexing

Spots #1 through #5 are muscle-relaxing exercises. You can't practice them too much. The more you practice, the more relaxed the muscles of the horse's neck get. The horse doesn't need to rest between gives. In fact, he gets better if you keep asking him to give in sets of 100, with only two-second intervals between the release and the next request. The motto we use for the first five spots is: **"More time giving, less time not."** That will help us remember to keep the horse giving, rather than him or us taking too many breaks.

The same is *not* true of Spots #6 through #9. Those spots are muscle-flexing or muscle-stressing exercises, and you can definitely overdo the practice there. These exercises ask the horse to work muscles that he normally doesn't work, so it's really important to give him breaks. In fact, you can improve his performance by giving him rest times of at least five seconds (10 seconds is better) between requests, allowing him to bring his head forward.

In beginning spots #6 through #9, the motto could be: **"More time resting, less time giving."** The release and rest are not pauses in the training; they are a significant part of the training. Remember that the release and rest are rewards for the horse, particularly when you are asking him to use muscles in a demanding manner. We don't want to make the horse "muscle sore;" we want to help him develop muscles that will enable him to carry his body in a more athletic manner, as we are teaching him to be responsive to our rein. With the first exercises, the rider gets into a pattern, and he can find himself lost in time. We don't want to carry that into the muscle stressing exercises.

Spot #6

Spot #6 is the first of the muscle-stressing exercises. The spot is physically located at the base of the horse's neck, where the neck joins the horse's body, but remember we're not just talking location; we're talking what happens there. The horse's performance of Spot #6 is critical to getting your horse to elevate his withers, so that he can float across the ground, rather than trudging along like he's wearing heavy boots.

Spot #6 in action will look as if Spot #1 — the jawbone — came toward the spot on the base of the horse's neck (see photo below). Up until now, the horse's neck has been relaxed and his nose has pointed to the side, essentially away from his body. Spot #6 is the first exercise that has the horse's neck, in effect, bow up, so that his nose comes back in toward his body. But it has to be done in a particular way, with the head to the side. This is not a matter of the horse breaking at the poll and bringing his nose to the center of his chest.

Spot #6 has two planes — one is horizontal, as if the horse were to bring his head toward your knee if you were in the saddle. The other is vertical — the horse will naturally bring his head farther down than you want. **Our goal will be to have him bring his jawbone toward the spot on the base of his neck and shoulder.**

But goals are not starting places. So, we'll ask for the "baby give," and we'll go through Spot #5. Up until now, we've done that by taking the slack out of the rein, bracing our hand against the saddle until the horse gives, then releasing the rein, using mini-releases to let the horse know he's on the right track.

This is one of the first times that the horse is "giving" Spot #6. Spot #1 — his jawbone — is moving toward where the base of his neck meets his shoulder, instead of just out to the side.

Here you can see the pretty arc of the horse's neck (Spot #3) and the livestock paint mark of Spot #6, though Seattle is nowhere near ready to perform Spot #6.

Once we are at Spot #5, with the horse's nose pointed, say left, we'll have to raise our rein hand, rather than leave it on the saddle. That's because we've been teaching the horse to give by moving his jawbone to the side. As he gets better at the "baby give," he's going to want to point his nose further out to the side, away from his body, or he's going to bring it around to our knee, if we're in the saddle. But we want it to move in, toward his shoulder. **Raising our hand will cause the horse to drop his nose in, toward the side of his chest.** You may actually have to push the horse's neck "forward" with the rein, to help him get the idea. At first, we'll only get slight movement, like a nod toward a fly down on that spot. When that happens, we should release, because the horse gave toward Spot #6. That's really all we are asking of him.

To explain Spot #6 another way, start out at Spot #1. Ask for "baby give, baby give, baby give" until the horse is at Spot #6. It may take 30 baby gives at two-second intervals to get there. Allow the horse to relax about 10 seconds and to take his nose out in front. Again go through the sequence until he ends up at Spot #6. It may only take 28 "baby gives" this time. Continue the process until it only takes a few gives until the horse brings his nose toward the spot on the base of his neck — Spot #6.

In these photos, Seattle is not giving, but has his neck out-stretched. John shows us the location of the four things we want to see happen when the horse "gives" in Spot #7.

First the bottom of the horse's neck, which we refer to as the fat part, will become the skinny part. And the skinny part (by the mane) will grow wide. As the horse's neck flexes, the upper neck muscles begin to carry his neck, rather than the lower ones just holding it up.

You'll get the impression that the horse's neck is attached to his body by way of a hinge. All of this takes training the muscles on the top of the neck to do a new job, the muscles on the "giving" side to contract and the muscles on the opposite side to entirely relax.

John's fist is in what we would call the "hole" that appears to develop. This is one indication of the relaxation of the under-neck muscles.

Spot #7

We want three things from Spot #7, and they happen in the same order. First, **wrinkles will develop in the skin of the horse's neck/shoulder area**. The wrinkles represent a surface softening of the muscle. Secondly, **there'll be what seems to be a hinge,** a line from the horse's mane down to Spot #6. It's like a new joint developed in his neck. Third, **a hole in the horse's neck appears to develop, as if the muscle disappears**

When these three things happen, the lower "fat" part of the horse's neck becomes the skinny part, and the skinny part (above the Spot #3 line) becomes the fatter part. Normally speaking, the crest area of the horse's neck is relatively thin. But a benefit of working on Spot #7 is that you will begin to develop the horse's topline.

Remember when Spot #3 — the big muscle along the horse's neck — formed a pretty curve? Well, when you work with Spot #7, you'll see Spot #3 take an arc like a rainbow, and it will seem that the horse is getting taller. You may find that the horse begins to shake his head — he's telling you that you are building a muscle, and it is uncomfortable. That's why it's important to give him breaks.

When you get Spot #6 consistently, you'll see Spot #7 begin to happen on its own, just as Spots #2 through #5 did. But, unlike #2 through #5, which we could have done at the standstill, we'll need forward motion for Spots #7 through #9. (Spots #2 through #5 are easier at the walk, but forward energy is *necessary* for the more advanced spots.)

Spot #8

When drawn on the horse, Spot #8 looks like an upside-down ice cream cone. In performance, when the horse gives with Spot #8, we are looking for two things. We want to see the muscles of the forearm begin to ripple. Second, we'll see a spot on the shoulder give and respond to the rein. **The result is that the opposite front leg usually steps in a forward/sideward movement.** Spot #8 doesn't come alive until you give it energy, so ask your horse to walk and go through #1 through #7. To get #8, you lift the rein, as you did for #6 and #7. This is the exercise we'll need to teach our horse to walk on the diagonal, and it will be invaluable for working on stepping into the canter or for lead changes. There are probably about a hundred reasons to work on diagonal movements, not the least of which is being able to slow your horse down.

John's hand is in the middle of the upside-down "v." You can see how it is farther back than Spot #6 (the hinge). When the horse is giving in Spot #8, his shoulder will move away from the rein. His foot may not move, but he'll shift his weight to the other shoulder.

For instance, let's take a horse who jigs on the trail. He's trotting nearly in place, getting increasingly excited. If we pull on both reins, he'll only get more excited and further stiffen his neck, which means he is less controllable. If we can tell him to soften his neck and to step his right shoulder toward the left, we can slow the horse's forward movement and get him to listen to our rein. Beyond that, by asking for the baby give, and having conditioned him to respond to our rein, by the time we are moving him diagonally, where is the elevation of his head? Of course, instead of his head being up and fighting the bit, it's at a relaxed elevation, which means the horse is also getting relaxed.

Spot #8 is where we begin to "connect the rein" to the feet, another concept in communicating through the reins. It's a term we use to describe picking up the rein and expecting the horse to move one of four major body parts — one shoulder or one hip. We'll discuss this more fully at another time, but it's helpful to begin to think about the concept. Instead of our rein talking to the horse's mouth, with practice, the horse will translate our rein requests to mean, "soften your jaw, relax your neck, elevate your withers, and move your shoulder or hip."

Spot #9

Spot #9 is up on the withers, and we want two things from it. **First, we want it to move directly to the left or right — not forward and not backward.** When Spot #9 gives, initially it feels like the horse is stepping to the side, but downhill, as if the saddle is falling off to the right, if you are working on the left rein. As you continue to train, it will feel as if the horse is stepping sideways on level ground. **Our goal with Spot #9 is to have the horse elevate his withers.** That will feel like the horse is going up a staircase to the right, if you are working on the left rein. He'll step up and over. It's what you want to feel when he steps into a lope, before a lead change or before you ask him for a stop.

As the withers elevate, the horse begins to carry more weight on his hindquarters. The front of the saddle will seem to rise, and when that happens as the horse's jaw is giving and his neck is soft, his back begins to round. That puts him in an excellent frame for carrying weight. It's the beginning of collection. With the front end light, the hindquarters can step under, and the horse can stop smoothly and in balance.

Through the rein

All this performance we're talking about happens with our talking to one side of the horse's mouth through the rein. Does that mean we never use two reins? No. It means that instead of distracting our horse from rein communication by using our seat, voice or leg aids, we are able to communicate precisely through each of two reins. So, once we've worked through all nine spots, we can ask for one thing from the left rein, and another from the right.

For instance, when we ask the horse to stop moving forward, we can pick up one rein, thinking about wanting him to stop, and he'll figure it out. Or, after training through these lessons, when we pick up the rein he'll "fast forward" through the spots until his front end elevates, at which point we can give him a little release and ask for the next movement.

Remember back to when you were learning to read, for instance, the word "see." When you first sounded it, you may have done a lot of sss'ing, and you felt a huge success when you got the whole word out successfully. Then, you combined the words, "See Spot run," reading one word at a time. Reading a whole sentence was heroic.

Now, we think nothing of zooming through much more complicated sentences without patting ourselves on the back with each one we read correctly. That's how it is with our horse. We are teaching him a new language and to "read" our communication, one sound and one word at a time. The "spot" training is teaching our horse a language, one word at a time. Once taught, the horse will understand when those words go together quickly to form a sentence. When he's learned the words and our pattern of speech, as it were, we can communicate in full sentences without him missing a beat.

Side benefits

When we work with this lesson in the riders' clinics, we typically start out with 15 horses who are all excited about being at a new place, many of them with real control problems. We have stallions as well as mares and gelding. None of them ground tie, and all are high as a kite. By the time we get done with the lesson, the horses have learned to ground tie — even though we haven't worked on it. The riders get off to come into the middle to watch something that I'm demonstrating. They get off, leaving the reins on the horse's neck so he won't step on them. They tell the horse to stay, the way one might tell a child not to cross the street, and walk away. Horses who were totally absorbed in the other horse activity stand relaxed. It's not just fatigue. They still have plenty of energy.

Somehow this systematic request-response-release provides the horse with some measure of calming down. It helps him screen out distractions and concentrate on one thing at a time. **These exercises develop not only the physical responsiveness of the horse and his mental recognition of your signals, but they encourage his emotional development as well.**

No harvest yet

Remember the farmer planting corn? Well, even though you'll be thrilled with the new level of responsiveness, none of this has anything to do with the horse's feet — the corn ready to pick. We're still just working on the corn plant, but now we have leaves, and Spots #8 and #9 are the ears of corn beginning to show up. The harvest is not far away. ▣

11

Making Connections

Once you've taught your horse to give to the bit and you've unlocked all nine spots, the next step is to "connect" the rein to the feet.

When we first established the "baby give," we began an arrangement with our horse that said, "When I pick up the rein, I expect you to relax your jaw and to move your head in the direction of that rein." The horse learned that as soon as he did what we asked, we released the rein. Thousands of repetitions later, when we pick up the rein, the horse doesn't have to think about what we want — he automatically relaxes his jaw and moves it in the direction we ask.

We know that any time a muscle stiffens, it's not available for work. So, a benefit of teaching our horse to give to the bit is that we developed a means of telling the horse to relax his jaw, then his poll, then the superficial muscles of his neck, the deeper muscles in his neck, the base of his neck and so forth. Because we want athletic performance from our horse, we conditioned him to relax all of those spots each time we pick up the rein.

So, how did we go from picking up the rein and asking one spot to give to the horse doing all those things each time we pick up the same rein? **When he "gave" with his jaw and we didn't completely release the rein, he said to himself, "There must be something else that my rider wants me to do." So he kept on giving.** Each time we gave him a mini-release. When he gave as deeply as we wanted, we gave him the full release. Then, because horses are so quick to understand a pattern, the horse learned to give all the way through the spots each time we picked up the rein.

When we got to Spots #8 and #9, no longer were we just asking him to bend his neck; we got the shoulders moving, too. We could say that we "connected" the rein to the horse's shoulders. That is, when we pick up the rein, thinking about Spots #8 and #9, instead of the rein talking to the horse's mouth, asking the mouth to do something, the mouth receives the signal, but it knows it can't answer the Spot #8 request. So the mouth is in a dilemma.

Remember back to what the horse wants most when we take the slack out of the rein? He wants us to release the rein. **Now, when we want the shoulder to move, there's nothing that the mouth can do to get us to release the rein. So, it sends a message to the shoulder to tell it to move, and fast.** The shoulder probably never had an independent thought in his life, so it was easy for him to take orders from the horse's mouth. The shoulder obeyed, and the mouth was rewarded for delivering the right message — we released the rein.

So now, instead of our having to physically talk to the shoulder — kicking it, bumping it, or worse yet, putting it off balance by some sudden body move — we can just send a message through the rein, by way of the mouth. We've connected the rein to the shoulder.

The mouth is a good messenger

We can use the same system to talk with any part of his body, because the mouth is always ready to tell somebody else to do something, so that he can get his rein released. Let's review the formula we use each time we want to ask our horse to perform a maneuver:
1) What is our motivator (why should the horse respond)?
2) What part of the horse's body do we want to talk to?
3) In what direction do we want that part to move?
4) How will we let the horse know when he did what we wanted (what's the payoff)?

Once we've taught the "giving to the bit" language, and we've started connecting the rein to various parts of the horse's body, we can almost always answer the first question with the same answer — the mouth wants us either not to pick up on the rein, or if we've taken the slack out of the rein, to let go of that rein. So we have a motivator that works for nearly everything.

Next, we figure out what part of the body we want to control or have change its movement, and what direction we want it to go. If the horse is running away with us, it's the hip pushing him forward. If we're leading the horse and he bangs into us with his left shoulder, then we want his left shoulder to move to the right (Spot #8 or #9).

Telling the horse that he guessed the right answer is as, or more, important than making the request. The less time between the horse's right move and your release, the faster he'll get the message that what he did was what you wanted.

If our horse is standing on the garden hose with his right hind foot, we can ask that foot to move to the left. In each case, we can do that without physically shoving the body part in the direction we want. We can pick up the rein, and politely tell the mouth what we'd like to have happen. The mouth will demand that the horse's body move as we've asked. And, without having broken a sweat, we can release the rein, thanking the mouth for its messenger service.

And, since we used the same motivator, we can use the same reward. The release is more valuable than dollar bills to the mouth.

Two type of connections

Essentially, you have two ways to teach the horse to make the rein connection, and the decision is up to whether you want great performance from your horse or just basic control. In both cases, we are talking about teaching the horse that the signal to move his body will come through the rein. We mentally connect the rein signal to the part of the body we want him to move.

Here John prepares to ask Seattle for a canter depart, setting him up by rein connections. Seattle's nose is pointing in the right direction, his neck is soft and his left hind foot is squarely under his body. In this position, he is balanced, and the first strides will be energetic, but will feel smooth to the rider.

If you want excellent control of your horse, and plan to do any type of sophisticated work, such as showing, working cattle, dressage and so forth, then you'll want to teach your horse to "give to the bit" all the way through the nine spots. That lets you ask the horse for collection, or ask him to elevate his shoulders so he can step off into the lope nicely. After that, you can "connect" the rein to the feet, allowing you to develop precise control.

However, the other option is to connect the rein to the feet just to develop basic control. We can teach him to mentally connect our use of the rein to his use of a part of his body. For instance, we could teach our green horse a useless thing like swishing his tail on cue, or something helpful, like stepping his right front foot to the right, so we can get him walking when he doesn't know to listen for our leg cue or when using our legs on him may cause him to get scared.

Just making the connections, without having taught the horse to give to the bit takes less time than teaching the horse to give to the bit and then connecting the rein to the feet — but the result is also far less polished. For instance, you can still ask your horse to canter, but it will be a lot rougher than if you taught him to give to the bit first, then connected the rein to the feet. You can put on the brakes and get the horse to stop, but it won't be the same balanced stop as if you had taught him that when you pick up the rein he should soften his jaw, neck, back and the joints of his legs

In the next chapter, we'll walk you through how to "connect" the reins to the horse's hip.

No Yellow Pages

Remember at the beginning of this "giving" discussion we talked about using the same phone to call all the contractors who were going to help us remodel the house? We used the Yellow Pages to know who to call for each job. Well, the yellow-pages analogy breaks down here — the horse has many parts, but we don't know what each does until we hire them. We have a general idea, but we have to take each part on trial to know how it works and what it does.

What we do know is that each part can move six directions — up, down, left, right, forward and back. And we know, now that we've developed a language that they all speak, that we can tell any part to go any direction. But knowing the benefits of engaging each part takes experimentation.

For instance, we know the hip pushes the horse forward. We know it's a powerful part, and it can work moving — such as when the horse runs — or in a balancing action — such as when a cutting horse follows the sudden movement of a cow. We know the hip can move up and power a kick, or move to the side to enable the horse to shy or sidepass. It can do subtle things, like accept more of the horse's weight, so he can lighten his front end to do collected work. We also know it can be off duty, as when you want a square stop but the horse stands like a slouch. So, how do we tell the hip what we want it to do?

We pick up the rein and slowly take all the slack out of it. We hold the rein steady, waiting for the horse to answer our call. If the horse knows the language, he'll recognize the rein as we would a ringing phone. He'll answer the call by softening his jawbone, then his neck and all the way back through the body until he softens the part we are calling — the hip. When the signal reaches the hip and he moves it, we'll release the rein, in effect hanging up. That release tells him that he did what we wanted. A split second later, we can pick up the phone and make another call, say, to the shoulder. The process repeats.

Teaching the horse maneuvers, such as walking on the diagonal, is stress-free, because the horse has already learned that the rein is just telling him where to put his feet, and when he guesses correctly, the rein will be released.

On the other hand, if our horse doesn't know the giving language, we can connect the rein directly. We'll use the same formula. The motivator will still be the slack taken out of the rein, and the reward the release. We'll walk you through a typical lesson in the next chapter, but the gist of it is that, by trial and error, the horse learns to move a particular part of his body. Unlike when he learned to give to the bit first, his movements may be stiff, and when the horse is under pressure, they may be quick, but not smooth. But, this is an effective way to gain control of a horse quickly — far more effective than trying to muscle him around. **I use this system when I'm riding a horse for the first time.** It gives me a way to gain control without adding intensity to a situation in which the horse might be already scared.

An important note: Once you've really made a connection to one of the four major parts of the horse — the shoulders and the hips — then you should not go back to working with just the baby give. Once the connection is made, you are telling your horse, "When I pick up the rein, I'm going to want you to give me a noticeable change in the position of at least one leg." If you go back to the baby give stage, in effect you'll be "disconnecting" the rein, telling the horse he doesn't have to move his feet when you pick up the rein.

Connecting on an "unbroke" horse

Imagine for a moment that you are sitting on a green horse for his first ride. You've done enough ground work, mounting and dismounting that he stands relaxed with you aboard. You naturally feel the urge to use your legs to ask him to go, but you know he hasn't learned what legs mean, and it would be counterproductive to start kicking this horse or making him uncomfortable in any way. Whatever you want him to do, you'll ask in a way that won't scare him. (He's already a bit scared, even if he doesn't show it.) And you want to do everything you can to make riding a pleasant experience for him. You are building a lifetime relationship.

With the horse standing still, we'll teach him the baby give, then we'll "connect" the rein to the horse's hip. Ideally, then, his first steps with us on board won't be

There's no fight in this case, though some horses pull pretty hard. Instead of pulling on the rein, this horse is just standing, thinking. Eventually, he'll move his hip when he can't take his nose forward.

forward, but to the side with his hindquarters. After several steps over with his hind feet, particularly when we connect the rein to each hip, he'll end up taking a few steps forward. When he stops walking forward, assuming that we want him to continue walking, we can ask his hips to move over, and then over again, until he begins walking. Then we'll leave him alone. He'll get the idea.

When I first worked an "unbroke" horse, I used to connect the rein to the horse's shoulders, asking the horse for a "baby give" deeper and deeper to one side until he finally moved one front foot. Then I'd switch to the other side. Eventually he'd move one front foot, then the other, until he ended up walking on his own. (That generally took me about 15 minutes.)

But, I discovered that connecting the rein to the hip instead of the shoulder is actually more effective. It reduces the time to get the horse moving and controllable, and it gives me a way to stop the horse if I have to. When I can control the horse's hip, I can turn or stop him. If I have the horse walking and he stops on his own, it's easier to get him walking again by moving his hip than his front feet. **PH**

12

"Hip" Talk

"Connecting" the rein to your horse's hip —
which really means the horse is "giving to the bit"
with his hip — gives you control over his first steps
and also opens the door to more advanced work.

How would you like to be able to tell your horse's right hip to go to the left, or his left hip to go to the right? You might wonder, what advantage could that possibly give you? After all, most riders are concerned about getting their horse to go, stop, turn or change speeds and leads, not about teaching their horse to hula. But, when we can control the horse's hips, we can:

- Get him to change directions.
- Position him for a controlled canter.
- Ask him to stop.
- Ask for a turn on the forehand.
- Get him to move on the diagonal.
- Begin the sidepass.
- Circle without his hindquarters drifting to the outside.
- Soften his shoulders, for smoother movements.
- And last, but not least, back up.

Before we go into the lesson, ask yourself, "Would it be easier to take directions from one person or from four people at the same time?" Obviously, just one. That's the thinking behind "connecting" one rein to the part of the horse's body we want him to move — instead of the horse trying to obey two reins, our two legs, our seat, weight and voice.

For this lesson, we're going to choose a spot on the top of the horse's left hip, and we'll ask it to go to the right. Why would we choose the

John asks Seattle to move his left hip to the right. Rather than irritate him with leg cues, John is teaching him to become more responsive to the rein.

hip instead of the horse's feet? Because it takes experience to know where the horse's feet are moving. With the hip, even beginners can concentrate and feel when it begins to move. We also want to reward our horse as early as we can, so he's encouraged.

This lesson isn't really hard for the horse, nor is it complicated, but it's difficult for the rider because it requires concentration. Don't let yourself be distracted by movements that the horse makes other than the one you want or by other horses outside your riding area. Don't be distracted if your horse calls to his friends or appears to ignore your request. You're not trying to "get his attention" — you're trying to get his hip to move in a certain direction. When the horse physically does what you want consistently, you'll gain his attention. **You really want control of his body; control of his mind will follow.** And, because you don't want to break your own concentration in order to steer, do this exercise in a safe enclosure, ideally without other horses. Assuming you are riding a horse who knows to walk forward when you ask, get the horse walking. It's easier to teach this lesson moving, because, like all lessons, we need movement.

Establishing a connection

Before connecting the rein to the hip, we will "connect" the rein to the jaw, and teach the horse to do a "baby give," as we did in earlier chapters. Either walking or standing, begin by asking for a baby give to the left. When the horse gives, release the rein. Count two seconds (one 1,000, two 1,000). Pick up the rein and ask again for a give. The second give comes quicker than the first.

After a number of gives to the left, with only a two-second pause between them, the horse will begin to leave his nose in the "give" position, instead of bringing his face forward again. That's good. At that point, switch reins, teaching the same lesson on the right. When he responds to both reins, switch sides every few minutes, until he gets consistent. When you can pick up the rein, take slack out of it and have the horse "give" within a few seconds, and when he does that consistently, you've "connected" the rein to the jawbone. The horse now knows that when you pick up the rein, you expect his jaw to move. (Getting the horse to this point usually takes me anywhere from 10 to 30 minutes on an "unbroke" horse.)

Making the hip connection

Now we will use that same language to connect the rein to the hip. We began by connecting the rein to the jawbone, because it's the easiest place to establish a connection. We use the jawbone to teach the horse the pattern — when you take all the slack out of the rein, he should move something, then you'll release the rein. And, just as you might relate something new to something you are already familiar with, when we release the rein after the horse moves his hip, he says, "Wait, we've done something like this before."

Take the slack out of the rein, as you did when asking for the "baby give," but this time thinking about the horse's left hip moving to the right. When the horse "gives" with his jawbone, release tension on the rein, but don't release the rein entirely.

So, now, with the horse's head off to one side, take the slack out of that rein, and hold slight tension on it until the left hip moves to the right. The horse may try to pull his head forward or down, in which case you should just hold the rein as you did before. He may "give" again with his jawbone, in which case you want to give him a mini-release, but then take the slack out of the rein again, continuing to think about him moving his hip.

Seattle gave with his jaw. John released tension on the rein, but didn't let the rein go. Seattle knows that when John doesn't "hang up the phone," he wants something additional. In this case, John wants Seattle to move his left hip to the right. In order to do that, Seattle first has to step the right hind foot over, to make room for the left.

Wanting relief from the confusion and, more importantly, relief from contact with his mouth, your horse will then explore options and eventually guess the right answer.

What happens if the horse gets upset enough that you feel unsafe? Then go back to asking him to "give" with his jaw, perhaps asking for bigger gives and allowing him more than two seconds between requests. That way, you can take the intensity out of the situation, without changing the language. When the horse is more solid at giving with his jaw, he'll be less excited as you graduate him from "connecting" the rein to his jaw to "connecting" the rein to his hip.

If your horse keeps giving his jawbone, you may end up with his head turned back by your leg. (We're not talking about Spot #2 here. We're saying he may end up like the horse on page 113 — not ideal, but acceptable temporarily.) Each time he gives, allow him a slight release so you are not pulling his head around, but not such a big release that he can swing his head forward. At this stage, the rein/bit is no longer the motivator, because there is probably no tension on the rein. The fact that the horse wants to take his head forward will motivate him to explore options. Eventually his neck will tire (just as it did in the round pen when the horse had his neck bent, looking at us with both eyes), and he'll move his feet.

No leg aids

When we do this exercise, it's tempting to use our legs to ask the horse to move sideways. Although that may get the horse to move, it doesn't teach him to be more responsive to the bridle, and it may generate some responses we don't want, like a stiffened neck or raised head. If we want responsiveness to the bit, we have to teach the horse to respond to the bit. Using leg, voice or seat aids distracts both the horse and ourselves from our focus on the bit. At a later time, we can add those aids, which will serve to add power or speed to the horse's response.

Waiting it out

Now the tricky part comes. You don't release when he begins to walk, or when he steps over with his shoulder. If the horse starts walking forward and then stops, you don't care. If he walks sideways, you aren't distracted. It's like you are a vending machine that only takes a certain kind of currency. **If he wants a loosened rein from you, the machine, then he needs to step his left hip to the right**. No other "coins" are accepted. You continue to think about the hip spot behind your left hip and continue to wait for that spot to move to the left. The moment it does, let the rein go.

When your horse finally does move his left hip to the right — even one small step — totally release the left rein. Count two seconds, then gather the left rein and ask the hip to move again. When you gather the rein, make sure you do so slowly and without bumping his mouth. Again, just maintain slight tension on the rein until the horse moves his left hip to the right. Do not kick him, or urge him in any way with your body. Just wait for the motivator to work. When you can pick up the left rein, thinking about the horse's left hip moving to the right, and his hip does just that, then you have "connected" the rein to the left hip.

As you might expect, the next step is to apply our same formula to connecting the right rein to the right hip. When you take slack out of the right rein, while thinking about the horse moving his right hip to the left, you are asking the horse to step to the left with his right hip.

Putting theory into practice

Now you can move the left hip to the right with the left rein, and the right hip to the left with the right rein. What else can we do with this lesson?

■ Imagine yourself on a trail ride, and your horse suddenly "locks up." Whether he hears a sound in the distance or just doesn't want to go any farther from home, his legs are planted and he's not moving. You've already asked him to go forward with your legs, and he has ignored your request. If you kick harder or start hitting him, you're afraid of an explosion. What can you do?

If you've "connected" the rein to the hip, you can tell his left hip to step to the right. That will break his stance. It may take moving that hip several times, but eventually you'll have the horse moving. If he heads in the wrong direction or he goes too fast, move the hip over again to gain control.

■ Imagine yourself wanting to go south on a north-bound horse. You've tried turning his head, but his feet are still going north. What can you do? If you've connected the rein to the hip, you can tell his left hip to move to the right, or southeast. As you repeat the request, the hip will move toward the east, then the northeast and, finally, the north. When the hip moves to the north, where is the horse's head pointing? South.

■ Imagine yourself trying to reach a snack sitting on a post of the arena fence. Each time you ride the horse up to the rail, his nose is near the snack, but his hindquarters are too far away for you to reach the rail with your left hand. Will you die of hunger or, worse yet, have to get off and then climb back on? Of course not. Just connect the right rein to the right hip and tell it to move over to the left — and snag your snack. This is the same problem many riders face when trying to open a gate on the trail.

So, we've used the same exercise to gain the basic control of our "unbroke" horse and to communicate more advanced maneuvers, like reaching a snack. What could be handier? ▣

Section III

Solutions To
Some Common
Riding Problems

13

Head Toss Cure

You say your horse tosses his head,
whether you have contact with the reins or not?
We'll show you how to end that dangerous habit,
once and for all.

When a horse tosses his head — flips his nose forward and raises his neck, usually in quick jerks — he endangers the rider. It can be scary to experience; people instinctively know that their horse is out of control. Those folks who are not frightened by the behavior are annoyed by it, and with good reason.

When a horse gets in the habit of tossing his head, it's often not long until his front feet leave the ground, and the horse then has a habit of rearing as well as head tossing. If the rider tries to limit the head tossing with a tie-down or forceful use of the reins, the horse often becomes more adamant, jigging or dancing sideways, and he gets harder and harder to control. Eventually, every time the rider touches the reins — no matter how lightly — the horse tries to jerk the reins out of the rider's grasp. Some horses end up pulling the rider forward as they flip their heads up, risking hitting the rider in the face with the back of their heads. (If you've merely felt inconvenienced by the problem but not taken it too seriously, ask some of the thousands of folk who've had broken noses or concussions because the horse hit them in their face.)

As frustrating and dangerous as the problem is, the solution is not complicated. It's easy to understand and easy to do, but it requires concentration on the part of the rider and lots of practice.

Unfortunately, we can't just tell a horse "don't" do something. And yelling at him, jerking on the reins or other attempts to punish his head tossing won't solve the problem. Anytime we want a horse to stop doing something, we have to replace what he's doing with something we'd rather he do instead.

Establish an objective

In the case of the horse who tosses his head, we have to tell him what we want him to do with his head. We want the horse's head at a particular elevation. We want him to respond to our use of the rein, to "give" his head to us when we request it. In time, he'll learn that every time he tosses his head we put his head to work, so it will become an easy decision to just keep his head relaxed.

We'll begin at the standstill or the walk to make it easiest for us and our horse, and we'll use a snaffle bit. While I prefer a full cheek snaffle, if you own a D-ring, eggbutt or O-ring snaffle, those would be fine to use. You don't want any kind of bit with a shank, even if it has a broken mouthpiece, such as a Tom Thumb. These are much more severe than a snaffle. We want the mildest bit we can use, and we'll teach the horse to obey it.

Just a word of advice: As long as the horse lives, he's going to have a tendency to pull on the bridle, just as every time you get in the car, you probably drive at least one mph over the speed limit. So, stronger bits aren't the answer — teaching him to respond to the mildest bit is.

Those people who have tried getting the horse to stop tossing his head by throwing away the reins know that doesn't work either. The horse has no motivation to change what he's doing. So, in order to get him to change his behavior, we have to motivate him to do so.

The motivator we use is our taking the slack out of the rein. When we take the slack out of one rein, the horse wants us to let go of the rein. So he experiments to see what will make us let go. If we are using the left rein, we want the horse to "give" his nose to the left. When he does, we'll let go of the rein. Until he does, we're going to brace our hand against the saddle so that he can't get our hand to move. If we let the horse move our hand, we're teaching him he can drag us around. We're also telling him to pull hard enough to get our hand to move. That's the opposite of what we want him to learn.

Asking for the give is a little tricky at first. You are going to only use one rein. Begin with the horse's head facing front. Slowly reach your left hand about halfway down the rein, close your fingers around the rein, and bring your left hand back to the saddle. If you move the horse's head with the rein, you've reached down too far and your rein has become too tight. If your rein doesn't have some tension on it when it's back at the saddle, pull the end of the rein with your right hand, sliding the rein through your left hand until the tension seems correct. You want only enough tension that the horse feels more than just light contact, but not so much tension that your rein moves the horse's head (that's his job).

So, now you've taken all the slack out of the rein, in effect, asking him a question. But, before landing on the right answer, he's likely to try a few wrong answers. When we use a full cheek snaffle and pull on the left rein, he feels pressure on the right side of his face. He's most likely going to push against that pressure, so we'll feel him pulling on the left rein as he tries to push the right cheek piece away. When that does not work, he'll likely raise his head, because that's what's worked in the past. **Generally speaking, horses learn that they can raise their heads and eliminate pressure on the bit, so that's always one of the first options they try.** If that doesn't work, the horse may pull down, may root his nose forward quickly (frequently one of the first options a head-tosser tries), tuck his nose toward his chest in a head-set-like position, or he may go into neutral.

Even with loose reins, a horse can root his nose forward. In that case, there is no motivation for him to change his behavior, so the rider will have to add pressure to one rein, asking the horse to give to the bit.

In the first photo, John pretends he's a horse and that his rider is pulling on the left rein. The natural reaction is to push against the right side of the cheek piece, in this case his finger. To the right, he's in "neutral." His cheek isn't putting any pressure on his finger, but neither is he responding to the bit by looking to the left.

Neutral on the rein is like neutral on a car — nothing's happening. The horse isn't pulling in any direction, but he's not giving, either. He may feel relief from the pull because he's put his head in a position where he doesn't feel a pull, but he doesn't have a release, and pretty soon he'll be pulling on the rein again. **When a horse goes into neutral, don't release the rein. If you do, you're telling him that neutral is what you want.** In fact, that's the reason that a number of horses with beautiful head sets are not in control. They go into neutral where they don't have any bit pressure, so consequently, they ignore the bit.

Ready to give

When the horse tries numerous options, one of them will be to move his head to the left. When he does, immediately release the rein. He'll wonder what he did to get the rein to release. We won't give him too much time to think about it, because in two seconds, we begin reaching for the left rein again and repeat the request. Again hold the rein locked against your saddle until he gives you the right answer. When you release, make sure you release the rein totally, so he feels a total reward.

If the horse doesn't give after what seems a reasonable time to you, try shortening the rein (without releasing it — just use your right hand to slide the rein through your left hand). Or, it could be that the rein is already too short. If your horse's head is turned very far to the left, he doesn't have anywhere to give.

It's going to take thousands of repetitions before the horse really knows what you want. You might walk along 80 times, releasing when his left jawbone gives, but he may also be stepping forward with his left hind foot. The eighty-first time, you might be standing still and ask him to give. He might step forward with his left hind foot, thinking he's got it right and going to get a reward. You won't release because he didn't give his jaw. He gets further confused, so he begins walking. You could easily become frustrated with him, thinking that he's being stubborn or ornery, when in fact he doesn't have a clue that you were talking to his jaw — not his left hind foot — the whole time.

REMEMBER, THE KEY TO CURING THE HEAD TOSSER IS TO STABILIZE YOUR HAND WHEN HE MOVES HIS HEAD AROUND.

So it will take working through lots of experiments, making sure you focus on just the jawbone and release the moment he energetically moves his head even a little bit to the left. The good part about all this is that once the horse gets the idea, you can do hundreds of repetitions in a short time. Counting will encourage you and help you stay on track.

Just a note: **If you are a person who is used to steering your horse a lot or who always wants your horse on the rail, you're going to have to ignore the frustration of not steering.** Since we can only concentrate on one thing at a time and we are using the rein to talk with the horse's jawbone, you really can't steer him through this process, which is why you'll want to practice initially in a safe, enclosed area. As you keep working on the left rein and the horse turns his nose to the left, he'll likely walk in circles to the left. If the circles get too small, just wait a longer time in between requests, and the horse will end up making the circles larger.

Now you have your horse giving to the left each time you pick up the rein. When this happens consistently, you'll also find that your horse's head is probably close to the elevation that you want. Next, you'll want to do the same lesson on the right rein. You'll find that the horse didn't transfer what he learned on the left to the right, but he'll know that you'll release when he does the right thing, so he'll put some effort into figuring out what you want. After lots of work on the right, you'll find that the right is better than the left, and so you'll go back to working on the left side again.

When the horse responds perfectly on both the left and right reins at the standstill and walk, then you can try asking him to give at the trot, and eventually at the canter.

Back to the head tosser

Having taught the horse this lesson, when the horse begins to toss his head, quickly pick up one rein, without bumping him with the bit, and stabilize your hand so he can't move it. Hold that rein steady the whole time he tosses his head. The moment he quits tossing his head and gives to you, release the rein. Not only are you teaching him what you want him to do, but he learns that every time he flips his head, you pick up on the rein — the very thing he'd prefer you not do.

John asks Seattle to give to the bit, then he releases the rein. If Seattle begins to toss his head again, John will ask him to give again and again, with only short intervals (one to two seconds) between requests, until Seattle relaxes his neck.

Seattle is pulling hard on the rein, and it doesn't look pretty. John has asked Seattle to give. Seattle swung his head to the left but immediately pulled it forward again. John's right hand immediately pulled the rein through the left hand to shorten it, asking Seattle to give again.

Remember, the key to curing the head tosser is to stabilize your hand when he moves his head around. Watch on the next trail ride, when you see a horse tossing his head. You'll see either slack in the rein, or the rider fighting with the horse's head, or the rider's hands moving around. In all three cases, the horse has no reason to keep his head quiet.

You can use this cue whenever the horse begins to toss his head, regardless of his speed or direction. Once you've taught him to give, the quicker you recognize that he's about to toss his head and you ask him to give, the better your overall control will be. Before long, as your horse becomes more and more responsive to the bit, you won't even remember having had a head-tossing problem.

Headshaking or head tossing?

There is a behavior known as headshaking in which the horse makes sudden nodding movements, tossing his head as if being attacked by a swarm of insects. This generally has nothing to do with avoiding the bit, as in the case of head tossing as our chapter discusses; instead, it's often an allergic or unusual neurological response, sometimes seen when the horse comes from a dark area into bright sunlight, and worse in the spring and summer. It can have any number of contributing causes. Should your horse have a pattern of acting like bees are after his face (but none are), call your veterinarian to come out to examine him. PH

Notes

14

Kicking On The Trail

If you're tired of warning everyone away from your horse and worrying about an accident on the trail, here's an explanation of what's happening and how to get your horse under your control.

Everything is fine when you are riding alone, but when another horse approaches yours on the trail, watch out — your horse turns into a kicking machine. **When you have a kicking horse and you want to end his kicking behavior, both the rider and horse have to go into training** — the rider to recognize the signs early and establish control, and the horse to learn to obey the rider. We'll discuss conditioning the rider to stay in charge, training the horse in a calm setting, then how to handle a potential kicking situation.

What won't work and why he kicks

Scolding a horse won't help. You can't punish a horse after he's kicked, and jerking on the reins only leads to unwanted behaviors, such as the horse throwing his head. An already scared and excited horse gets more excited when he feels he has to fight you and the other horse, too.

You see, many horses kick other horses because they are afraid. It's rarely the alpha horse who kicks; instead, it's usually the horse at the bottom end of the pecking order or the horse who normally lives alone. Sometimes what happens is that two horses buddy up when on the trailer, then the lowest-ranking horse tries to keep the other horses away from his new friend.

This is the goal: To be able to ride along on a loose rein and not worry about one horse kicking another. But, a goal is not a starting place, and the time to control your horse's kicking behavior is not when another horse is at his tail.

The kicking horse becomes increasingly focused on the other horses, often insisting on going where he wants and ignoring his rider. Solving the kicking problem often involves more than just kicking behavior; it involves helping the horse develop emotional control, as well as the rider learning how to prevent a kick.

Active or reactive rider

Before you can get the horse under control, you have to determine that you're going to be the active partner, rather than the reactive one. **Whoever is active gains the other person's attention.** In this case, the other person is your horse.

So when your horse tries to kick another horse and you correct him, he's the active partner — the one initiating an action — and you're the reactive one. You are responding to his behavior. In order to deal with the kicking horse, we have to reverse those roles: If you wait until he's ready to kick or has kicked, you are too late.

Imagine for a moment being really engrossed in watching a movie. Someone might walk into the room and you wouldn't even notice it. When they finally get your attention, you might be startled that they were there. The kicking horse isn't watching a movie, but he's living in a real-life drama, engrossed in watching what other horses are doing. He barely notices you (you already know that), and when he finally does because you've become insistent, he might respond in a startled or irritated way, because you are distracting him from the other horses, which may put him in danger. Remember, he's probably the low man on the totem pole, so to speak, so he watches out for any horse who might even think of bullying or intimidating him.

In order for the horse to pay attention to us, we have to become more important to him than the other horses. And, we can't do that by force. **We have to replace his worry and preoccupation with the other horses with his conditioned response to our cues.**

Establishing control

As with anything we want to teach our horse, we have to train the physical, mental and emotional parts of him. Normally, we try to approach any lesson so that we train one-third of each. **But, kicking other horses is more an emotional response than a mental or physical one, so we'll concentrate more than one-third of the training in that area.** Realizing that you are working with the horse's emotions helps you to stay focused and not get upset with the horse. He's not trying to be difficult, rude or rebellious; he just needs training to respond better to what you want him to do.

The rule we follow is: Go to a place in the training where you can ask the horse to do something and have him do it 100 percent of the time. So that's where we'll start. It might be riding alone in an arena at the walk. Pick one exercise, or a series of related exercises, and work on those until your horse is responding consistently. Keep your standards high. Most people think that their horse is under control until the moment he is radically out of control. In reality, he may have been technically out of control for quite a while.

Work on that one exercise, say, giving to the bit or walk-stop-walk-trot-walk transitions, until you are sure that he's 100 percent focused on you. How will you know that? His performance will become consistent — he'll seem to almost be able to read your mind. To get that level of performance, you'll have to focus 100 percent on the exercise, too, and become 100 percent consistent in your signals and releases. You'll have to give him your undivided attention if you expect his.

Once you've developed good control of your horse without any other horses around, have someone casually ride near you. Notice that Zip is alert, but John has him focused on moving forward, not reacting to the other horse.

Introducing another horse

When your horse is working up to par, ask another rider to ride toward you, but not too close. Immediately speed up your cue, asking him for more performance, perhaps a change in leg speed (up or down) or a turn. While ignoring the other horse, keep the standard of performance that you expect from your horse as high as it was when you were practicing alone. Work only on familiar lessons while the other horse just works around the area — not directly invading your horse's space or challenging him in any way. Your goal is to improve your horse's mental recognition of your cue and his conditioned response to it. But, more importantly, you will train his emotions at the same time.

There is a physical component to training the emotions. Each time a horse comes near him, your horse's heart rate goes up. You can recognize that by the tension in his neck and perhaps a stiffening of his body. The same thing may occur when his buddy horse goes out of sight. You want to put him in a situation where his heart rate goes up a little bit, but not so much that his fear becomes the driving force in the moment. You want him to respond to your cues at the same time — so he learns he can live with a little fear and still perform. The result is that his heart rate will go down again, particularly when the other horse goes away.

That up and down of his anxiety level is tiring, and with enough repetition, the horse will figure out that it is easier for him to stay relaxed than to get upset and have to calm down again.

Adding excitement

What if you keep your horse by himself, so the problem of kicking other horses only surfaces on a trail ride? There are several ways to increase the horse's excitement level so you can practice at home. One is with the addition of exciting distractions, such as the feed cart, maybe a child on a bicycle, someone kicking a bucket around and so forth. The other way is by adding speed.

You'll find that your horse may respond perfectly at the walk, but at the trot, he's hard to manage. He's hard to control because he's excited — the very element you want to add to your training program. So, go from walk to trot, planning to ask him back to go back to the walk after a certain number of strides. You can vary this according to how well controlled your horse is, but only trot as many steps as you can control safely.

John asks Zip to give to the bit and to move his shoulders closer to the other horse. Horses who kick on the trail may also tend to bite at other horses. The better you've trained your horse to "give," the better control you'll have of his shoulders and hindquarters.

When John thinks that Zip is about to act ugly toward the other horse, he asks Zip to give to the left — toward the other horse. That will move Zip's hindquarters to the right, and hopefully out of kicking range. Note that the other rider asks her horse to give, keeping his attention focused on her and avoiding aggravating Zip.

So if you know after 20 steps he's free-wheeling, at 10 steps begin to ask him to come back to the walk. Then walk, asking him to give to the bit, circle or make a series of S-turns. When he's calm and under control, you can think about adding excitement again. The move from trot to canter is even more exciting than from walk to trot.

The rule we follow is: **Ride where you can, not where you can't.** "Where" doesn't just mean location— it also means speed (fast trot/slow trot), gait (walk/trot/canter), environment, number of horses around, how you're feeling, etc. You only want to practice being in control, so that may mean limiting your activities until he's super under-control before doing more exciting maneuvers or putting him in more stimulating circumstances.

Remember that your objective is to get the horse's heart rate slightly elevated, but not so high that he can't respond correctly to your requests. It doesn't matter if he hollers to his friends, as long as he's physically doing what you ask. When you ignore his hollering and concentrate on the exercise, he'll quit hollering and respond better to your cues, and you'll find his "attention" will be focused on you.

Staying the active partner

Through all of this, you are going to be the active partner, not reacting to what your horse does, but consistently asking him for specific performance. That's easier said than done. If you pay attention to the person kicking a bucket around, then you are probably as, or more, distracted than the horse. **The person who can keep his mind on one thing the longest becomes the active partner.** Ignore the horse's undesirable behavior and stay focused on what you are asking him to do. If he changes his behavior, and you try to "correct" his bad behavior, you've become reactive, and the horse is determining your actions.

Let's say that you are working on making left and right turns, and the horse gets excited. He speeds up, stiffening his neck, making turning more difficult. What should you do?

If you've been asking him to give to the bit as you are making the turns, you can shorten the time between requests. So instead of asking for a give about every five seconds, ask him the moment his neck straightens out, say, every two seconds.

Eventually work up to being able to ride past each other, keeping both horses under control. Note that Zip isn't happy (see his tail), but he's not attempting to kick the other horse, and John isn't having to call his attention back. In addition to improving their horses' performances, the riders are having fun.

Putting an exercise into play

You've developed the skills you'll need — your concentration and his performance in calm and exciting circumstances. Now for the test. You are going to set up a situation of a potential kick, but you are going to avoid the kick, by keeping your horse too busy to notice the other horse. With a responsible riding buddy, both of you work on circling, coming closer to each other from time to time. When your horse appears irritated with the other horse — swishing his tail, tensing his neck or laying an ear back— immediately turn his head toward the other horse, which turns his hindquarters away. Bring him to a stop. (You may have to use one rein, then the other, if your horse tries to lunge toward the other horse.) Allow the other horse to go by. Resume circling, keeping the horses far enough apart that you don't compromise safety or the good performance you worked on earlier. If you are riding close enough that the horses are hard to steer, you're too close.

When the other horse approaches yours, turn your horse so his hindquarters swing away from the other horse again, and keep him focused on what you want him to do. As you approach use a request-give-release pattern rather than just riding with relatively loose reins waiting to see what's going to happen.

We want the horse to be so busy answering our requests that he doesn't have time or energy to think about the other horse. We'll replace his ugly behavior with behavior we want. And, in time, he'll learn the other horse isn't a threat. You'll have developed good control of him, and you'll have trained yourself to recognize the signs of an impending kick long before it happens. And, you might just exchange that red ribbon in his tail (to warn other riders away from your kicking horse) for a blue ribbon in trail riding. PH

15

Pre-Ride Check Out

You've been invited to ride a friend's horse,
but you are concerned you may not be able
to control the borrowed horse.
What can you do to help assure you have a safe ride?

W e all love to be invited somewhere. But when that invitation includes riding an unknown horse, we have to take special precautions. First, I'll tell you how to do a pre-ride check, so you'll know as best you can what you are dealing with and if taking a ride is even a good idea. Then, if you decide riding is safe but would like an extra amount of control, you may want to "connect the rein to the hip."

Owner info

Ask the owner to tell you about his horse. Listen carefully for words that don't seem as if they should apply to horses. For instance, if the horse is reported to be "handy with his feet," that may mean anything from, "He's going to kick your brains out when you try to catch him" to "He's sure-footed on the trail." Likewise, if they tell you, "He's fine with other horses," that may mean either he doesn't have any undesirable habits, like kicking other horses on the trail, or it could mean that he doesn't have any brakes — he only stops when the other horses stop. So, explore beyond the superficial description.

Next, ask the person about the equipment the horse usually wears. If, for instance, the horse has always been ridden English, he may not be used to the back cinch of your Western saddle, and a tightly

Ask questions, but don't believe everything someone tells you about their horse. You are always the one responsible for your own safety.

adjusted martingale or tie-down may indicate that the horse has a head-tossing problem. But, the equipment won't solve the problem, and the horse may fight the equipment itself.

If the owner uses a whomper-stomper bit, try to find out why it's needed. In many cases, it's just the bit that the horse came with when he bought him. or it's all the owner knows to use.

Ask how long it's been since the horse has been ridden, or been ridden off the farm. He may have been a show stopper in his time, but he may be a ride stopper today, if he hasn't been ridden for the last five years or he's overly worried about his buddy.

Do your own research

Carefully observe the owner with the horse. Does the owner seem confident, handling the horse easily, or does he seem afraid, treating the horse like an explosion waiting to happen? Beyond that, does the owner set boundaries for the horse? For instance, walking down a barn aisle, does he require the horse to walk alongside him, or is the horse on a long lead rope and visiting each horse along the way? Who "owns" the owner's space? **Is the horse respectful of the owner's space, or does the owner step out of the horse's way?**

Watch as the owner grooms the horse. Do they seem to get along, or is one always picking on the other? Is the horse a fusspot, stomping his foot the moment the owner walks away? If so, he's more likely to be fussy on the trail as well, perhaps not having developed much emotional control.

When the owner asks the horse to do something, like move over or pick up a foot, how does the horse respond? An ears-back, tail-swishing response may tell you the horse isn't in the habit of co-operating with the owner, or that the owner is in the habit of using irritating cues.

Does the horse stand tied? For instance, did the owner tie the horse as you would a well-trained horse, or did he use a hay string, so the horse wouldn't hurt himself tied, or worse yet, ask you to hold the horse so he did not have to tie him up? If the horse doesn't stand tied, he's likely not learned to "give" to pressure, which means that he won't "give" to your rein very easily, either.

Is there any indication that the horse is headshy? Headshy

Observe the owner riding the horse. Note particularly his attitude. Are they having fun? Does the horse seem easy to control?

horses are dangerous. If the horse won't tolerate someone reaching for his head or ears without flinching in a big way, he's likely not to tolerate a branch near his head, or your tissue blowing away, or your right hand reaching to scratch your head when you are in the saddle, for that matter.

Does the owner insist on turning the horse out, or lungeing him, before you ride? Some owners do that as a matter of course — a warm-up for stall-bound horses. But for others, they are hoping that blowing off a little energy will substitute for good training.

Now to tacking up. Watch for signs of cinchiness or overall crabbiness. See if the horse opens his mouth willingly for the bridle.

Making decisions

Now summon lots of courage, and ask the owner to ride the horse for you. If he won't, you shouldn't either. Politely refuse to ride. **I never get on a horse that I haven't either started myself or seen ridden by someone else.** I never take anyone at their word when they tell me the horse is trained, because I can't know for sure what they mean by "trained."

A word of warning: People are free with your seat. They often pre-sume that you will have better success with a horse than they have had. I know folks see me as disposable. They tell me face-to-face how much they appreciate me and my teaching, then hand me ol' Widow-Maker to ride. Somehow, they think that I'm going to be able to ride an untrained horse better or more safely than they can. Because I work with so many green horses, I might last longer on his back than someone else, but I wouldn't be doing myself, them or the horse any good by asking him to do something that he's not ready to do.

If the horse is headshy, cinchy or known to buck, I don't get on him. I work with those problems from the ground — where we both can stay safe, and where the horse has an easier job of learning.

The horse's report

In the words of the famous Mr. Ed, "Go right to the source, and ask the horse..." Approach the horse in a confident, friendly manner, and take him for a little walk. Leading him 50 feet away from the barn can tell you a lot about his manners. Note particularly if he stops when you stop, and if he pulls on the lead when you take the slack out of it. **If he pulls against you on the lead rope, I can al-most guarantee that he'll pull against you when you take slack out of the rein.** If he stops easily, waiting for your cue, you've got a much better chance of having a horse who listens to rein signals.

As you watch the owner riding, see what signals he uses to communicate what he wants to the horse, and how he tells the horse that he did the right thing. Observe how the horse reacts to distractions. Obviously, this horse doesn't mind dogs running around. That's important to know if you are planning to take the dogs along on the trail.

If he's really rude, pulling you over to a patch of grass, or knocking into you with his head, then

Put the horse through a few tests. When you lead him, does he crowd you or respect your space? When you flap a saddle blanket, does the horse have a big reaction or take it in stride? This horse hasn't been taught to "spook in place," that is, to turn to face a spooky object. But, he's not overly spooky, doing the natural thing for a calm, trail horse to do, which is just to turn aside. Note that he's not pulling away. That's a good sign.

you can expect an even lower level of obedience under saddle, especially when he gets excited.

Check your bridle and girth. When you feel ready to ride, step aboard in an area where you'll feel safe. Look to get along with the horse, and see how light a cue you can use and still have the horse respond. After all, this is his first ride with you, too. You don't want to start out picking a fight.

Once you have your bearings, have walked around a bit and feel confident, ask the horse to go forward using leg cues, not your voice, rein or weight. Why leg cues? Because you want to know if the horse responds to leg cues. When you are on the trail and have to urge the horse to go forward — say, across a ditch — voice and weight cues may not be sufficient.

But, before you get going too fast, test the brakes. Is the horse trained to a one-rein or a two-rein stop cue? Does he respond to either? How easy is it to turn him?

Then test ride the horse at various speeds. Old Pokey may be very controllable at slow speeds, but if something scares him, if he gets going faster than he's accustomed to going, how controllable will he be? Begin by asking him to go into the trot. Notice if he goes forward smoothly or bolts forward. Then, does he hold that speed, or speed up and slow down without your signalling him? If so, he may be used to making decisions for himself, instead of staying in a gait until the rider gives him a next signal. When he goes faster, does his head stay at the same elevation, or does it appear he's scanning the sky for birds? If his head went up, you know his heart rate did, also (as yours might have, also). The higher his head, the less control you'll have.

Can you ask him to drop his head ("calm down" cue)? Take all the slack out of one rein and hold it against the saddle. The horse may turn, pull his head one way or the other, but when he lowers his ear one-half inch, then release the rein. A few times like this will tell you how easy it will be to get the horse to drop his head and calm down should the need arise.

Be sure to ride at various speeds. The horse who performs perfectly at the walk may get pretty excited at the trot or canter and be much harder to control. On the other hand, if you've tested him at all gaits, you will be that much more confident out on the trail.

The pre-ride check out is a pass-fail test in the sense that it decides if you'll take the horse out on a ride. Even so, it should be a positive experience for both you and the horse. Be sure to encourage the horse often.

If you are riding a horse who knows canter departs, then just ask him to step into the canter from the walk or jog. If not, ask him to trot with longer and longer steps, until he breaks into a canter. Again evaluate the control you have. Ask him to stop from the canter.

If at any point along the way, you think that you shouldn't ride the horse, *you shouldn't ride the horse.* No one can make that decision for you. Your safety is always your responsibility. Take whatever safety precautions you think are feasible — including wearing the right gear and a helmet. When we make compromises ("It will be OK just this once"), we are speaking hopefully — and dangerously. ■

Notes

16

It's A Cinch

The answer to the problem
of saddling a cinchy horse is
to program the horse to know there's relief.

hen a horse is bugged by a fly on his back, he may bite at the fly, but the fly is usually long gone by the time the horse's mouth gets to the scene of the bite. The horse goes back to grazing or whatever he was doing. He doesn't stay mad at the fly.

We're going to approach the cinchy-horse problem as if the cinch were a fly. We're going to apply cinch pressure for a second, then release it before the horse has had time to react.

When we talk about the horse being cinchy, we mean that he dances around or gets anxious, pulls back, or otherwise registers his extreme displeasure or fear at the saddle being cinched or girthed up. Cinchy horses are dangerous — both to themselves and to people.

The usual method of dealing with this problem is, with the horse not standing tied, to slowly ease the cinch tighter and tighter, walking the horse a few steps in between tightenings. This method occasionally gets you by but doesn't solve the problem.

The danger comes when a person saddling the horse leaves the cinch loose, then ties the horse. It's very easy for someone not knowing the problem or not thinking about it to tighten the cinch in the usual manner and have the horse pull back or come unglued in some other way. If you have a cinchy horse, you should work with the problem until the horse is no longer cinchy.

Start out in a round pen or safe enclosure. Do not tie the horse but do put on a halter and lead rope, and have another rope handy.

Stand well to the front of the horse, as you see John doing.

For this lesson, we'll assume that your horse has been sacked out and is comfortable being handled and is safe to work around; he's just cinchy.

Obviously, saddling requires that your horse stand still, and so does this exercise. If the horse moves around, ask him to stand. If he doesn't stand, give him a job to do, like backing or walking forward and then to the side. After about a minute of work, give the horse the opportunity to stand again. After a few times, he'll get the idea that it's easier to stand still than to do the exercises you have as an alternative. Make sure the horse is comfortable with one step before going on to the next.

1. Approach the horse's left shoulder, pet him with your right hand, then step away. When we tell you to walk or step away, we mean just two or three feet, still holding the lead rope. It's a way of telling the horse that he's off the hook: Session's ended. You'll begin another session again in a few seconds, but he's not concerned with that.

2. Pet the horse with your right hand, run it over his back and sides, then step away.

3. Pet the horse all over his back and sides with the rope in your right hand, then step away.

4. Reach your right hand (and rope) over the horse's back and give him a firm, quick hug. Step away.

5. Reach over the horse's back with your right hand and reach under his girth area with your left. Give him a quick, very firm hug; then release quickly and step away. When you do this, be sure that you are standing in a safe position — just a reminder that horses can and do kick forward with a hind foot, and you don't want to be caught in the line of fire.

6. Petting the horse as before, drop the rope over the horse's back as if it were the cinch, reach underneath, pick up the rope, pull it snug quickly, then release it — as if a fly just bit your horse and then evaporated. For this reason you do NOT want to do this step slowly.

7. Repeat Step 6 until the horse stands comfortably, as if he doesn't even notice that you are snugging the rope up under his belly.

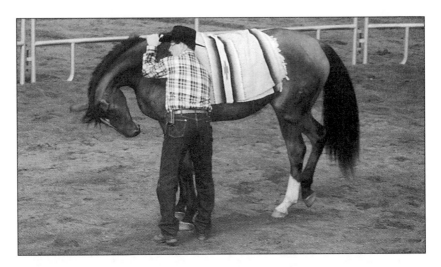

Many cinchy problems have their root in other problems. This horse has never been ridden, yet he is clearly telling John he's not comfortable with John's hand down by his girth. No sense proceeding to the saddle until he's feeling secure with this step; that would only intensify the wreck.

8. Put the saddle blanket on the horse, then the saddle. If at any point the horse shows resistance, that tells you to go back to sacking-out and saddling exercises. Stand facing the horse's left shoulder, as far forward as you can and still be able to reach the cinch with your right hand. Grasp the cinch, pull it up quickly to your horse's belly, then release it quickly. Step away.

9. Bring the cinch up quickly, almost slapping it against the horse's belly, as you did on Step 8, but hold it about three seconds this time before you release.

10. When the horse doesn't appear to mind Step 9, increase the time until you can hold the girth up there for about 20 seconds without the horse squirming around.

11. Run the latigo through the cinch ring once. Take the slack out of the cinch quickly, bringing it up to touch the horse's belly, then release it immediately.

12. Gradually increase the time the cinch is holding pressure against the horse's girth area, as you did with the rope. You still have a safety valve — you can release the latigo if the horse gets upset. When the horse can stand comfortably, you should be ready to continue the saddling procedure.

Pull the latigo quickly, and release it immediately. You want to time it so that cinch pressure is gone long before the horse has time to react.

The rule is: Go to a point in the training where you can ask the horse to do something and have him do it 100 percent of the time. A horse with a leading, headshyness or pulling-back problem will often be cinchy. Establish good leading manners and teach your horse to yield to pressure on the lead rope before beginning advanced sacking out or saddling.

13. After the saddle is secure, take the halter and lead off and step quickly away from the horse at a 45-degree angle in case he bucks. Ask him to move around for several minutes so that you are sure he's OK with the saddle.

14. Repeat the entire exercise from the beginning about 20 or 30 times. After the first time or two, it is not necessary to ask him to move around the corral, just take the saddle and blanket off, put them on and cinch him up firmly.

You may need to do this exercise for a few days, but whenever you cinch up your horse, be sure to do it matter-of-factly, not gingerly, and have the saddle secure. Before long, you'll make saddling just a part of your horse's everyday life. **PH**

Notes

Section IV

Putting Theory
Into Practice

17

Natural Isn't Always Best

*If you want to confuse your horse, let him do
what comes naturally — but then don't expect him
to win a ribbon, or to obey you on a trail ride.
You'll learn that "natural" isn't all it's cracked up to be.*

We like the idea of natural. We somehow feel that natural is better than the alternative — for instance, that natural foods are better for you than "unnatural" or artificial foods. Applying that line of thinking to everything, which is the natural thing to do, can get us into trouble. In fact, most of the time, we do not really want either ourselves or our horses to just act naturally. And, natural implies "easy." But learning new ways of behavior isn't easy. Let's look at some things our horses do and what response we'd like from them.

Reactions vs. conditioned response

Let's think about the natural response. Cat sees dog. Dog sees cat. Dog looks like he's going to chase cat. Cat, thinking naturally, runs. But the wise old cat, the one who has learned not to react naturally, thinks, "If I sit here looking at that stupid dog, he won't chase me." **It's not natural for cats to sit still when they think a dog may chase them, but education is often more valuable than natural reaction.**

What's more natural for a prey animal than to run when startled? Yet, we want our horses to replace that "Flee first, ask questions later" instinct with a learned response — or else we'll find ourselves on the hard ground.

When a bear roars, it isn't natural for a horse to stand calmly watching him. Of course, it isn't natural for the horse trainer to just stand there, either.

Herd-type behavior falls into the same category. I wish I could tell you the number of people who tell me that their horse responds perfectly in the arena, but that he is uncontrollable on the trail when the other horses begin to run or act up. I could console them by telling them their horse is just acting naturally, but that wouldn't help much. They want to know how to deal with that "natural" behavior.

It's natural to think that if we want our horses to do something, we should talk horse language. But, our goal isn't to join the herd; we want our horses to function in our world. So, if we want them to do the unnatural, we have to do the unnatural — we have to teach them a new language, which is what training is all about.

Resisting pressure

When we push on our horse's hip, say, to move him over, it's natural for him to lean against us. We want him to move away from pressure, but he naturally moves into it.

One of the things that novice horse handlers learn — often the hard way — is that you can "lead" a horse, but you can't "pull" him along. When a person pulls on a lead line, thinking they'll force a horse to step forward — for instance, to go into a horse trailer — what happens?

The horse doesn't go forward, but backward. The halter puts pressure on the top of the horse's head, and instead of his moving forward to relieve the pressure, the horse does what comes naturally — he meets pressure with pressure. Moving forward — relieving pressure instead of overpowering it — is a learned response.

And, why do we get so frustrated with horses who drag us off on the lead rope? We presume that because the horse may generally follow us around the pasture (we think we're leading him), he's been taught to obey the lead rope. In 90 percent of the cases, the horse hasn't been taught leading cues. So when something distracts him and we pull on the lead rope in an attempt to get him back on our agenda, he does the natural thing — he pulls on his end of the lead rope.

The same principle applies to working with the bridle. When we pull on a rein, it's natural for the horse to pull against us — to lean on the bit. That tendency is really strong, and it's something you'll see at play throughout a horse's entire life — even in well-trained horses. We go to great lengths to teach the horse that when we pull on the rein, we want him not only to not pull against us, but to relax his neck and yield his mouth to us.

Traveling naturally

Some people think that we don't really "teach" the horse to do anything — that everything we ask of him is really a natural maneuver, and that all we have to do is establish a language that communicates to him which movement we want him to do. But I don't really think we want our horses traveling naturally.

Horses may naturally "collect" out in the pasture, but not for long — three or four strides to rebalance, then a change of speed. It isn't natural for a horse to travel in a collected manner for very long, particularly the way many western pleasure horses do, looking at the ground. And, while a horse may have a spectacular extended trot in the pasture, after five or six strides, he'll usually either canter or stop.

Then, too, what horse would naturally step into a tire on the ground out on the trail, like a "trail horse"? **So, does it mean that when we ask the horse to do something unnatural, it's bad for the horse? No. In many cases we ask him to do the trained or unnatural thing for his own good.** Take head carriage, for instance.

The untrained horse automatically travels with his head "up." As a result, his back looks swayback (hollow). We know that when a horse's back is in that position, his weight-carrying capacity is diminished, making it harder to balance himself under a rider. Then,

*We can use natural behavior to initially establish communication,
but performance requires replacing "natural" with "learned."*

too, his feet hit the ground harder, causing extra concussion on his
legs and feet, and making it harder for the rider to sit quietly on him.
And, he's also far more likely to hit one leg with another foot. Not
to mention that, when the horse's head is up, he's much more likely
to react in a big way to anything unexpected.

So, what unnatural thing do we ask him to do? We ask him to
lower his head, straighten his back and step underneath himself
with his back feet. This allows his back to support weight, instead
of acting like a suspension bridge. It means he'll be more comfortable to ride, and he will probably stay sound for a longer period.

And, how about stepping into a tire, or walking over a teeter-totter
bridge? By asking the horse to do something unnatural, we can test
how well he understands our specific cues.

In fact, the whole concept of responding to cues doesn't come naturally. We use the horse's natural ability to recognize patterns, but
then we ask him to recognize highly unnatural patterns.

Of course, we could go on at length about how unnatural it is for
the horse to travel in circles or to stand still as we mount, but then
we'd be pointing out the obvious, which is the natural thing for
people to do — so we'll avoid that trap. But, what other natural tendencies do we deal with?

The natural rider

Just as the horse reacts physically, mentally and emotionally, our natural reactions in those areas sometimes don't serve us best. That's true even regarding the physical part of riding. When our horse is going too fast, our inclination to grip with our legs and tighten both reins can get us into real trouble.

Emotionally speaking, it's natural for us to take it personally when a horse doesn't do what we want him to do, but horses don't do things with the idea of embarrassing us.

And, because a horse has responded correctly to a request a few times, our natural presumption that he's learned the lesson will lead us to be frustrated with his natural behavior.

It's not natural to think in terms of rewarding the horse; it's far more natural to think in terms of being demanding. But we don't get consistent performance from our horse until we realize that he'll do a maneuver a million times for a million rewards, but only a few times for just a demand. Even when we think we understand that concept, when we find ourselves in a tight spot, we tend to intensify the demand; we rarely show the horse that a reward is in the offing.

Which brings us to the point of consistency. **It's normal to assume that we are consistent in our behavior, but a reality check would tell us otherwise** — and our horse's inconsistent performance tells us we both tend to be inconsistent.

Using equipment

When the horse doesn't seem to be doing what we want, it's natural to use mechanical help. After all, he's bigger than we are, so a little leverage goes a long way. Right? Wrong, in most cases. Does a more severe bit stop a horse? Rarely. It may intimidate him a time or two, but adding pain won't train the horse; it will only distract him from his job.

And, if someone poked you in the side with a stick, would you think about stepping sideways? Yet, we presume that if we wear bigger spurs, our horse will naturally get the idea to move over.

How about using gadgets, such as tie-downs, to get the horse's head in the right spot? Again, it's natural to think those will work; but, they don't help produce a better-trained horse.

How about confining a scared horse who wants to escape? That's a wreck waiting to happen.

And, it's natural for us to use the reins to discipline the horse. We instinctively jerk on the rein or lead rope to express our frustration and to tell the horse to pay attention to us. But, a quick look at the results of our action tells us that the natural thing is also the worst thing.

Instead of the horse trusting our leadership, he looks at us as something to be feared, not trusted. And, of course, instead of getting the behavior we want, we force behavior we don't want, such as the horse throwing his head in the air, stiffening his neck and preparing his body for escape, not compliance. Riders who have worked at developing "good hands" will tell you that using the reins or lead rope as communication devices doesn't come naturally.

In moments of pressure

Probably nothing reveals natural tendencies better than when our reactions bypass our thinking, such as in intense moments.

When I'm teaching clinics, one of the hardest things for people to learn to do is to let go of the rein for a moment. They naturally think that releasing the rein on a nearly out-of-control horse means that the horse will be further out of control. But the reverse is generally true. When they release the rein for a moment, the horse

Experts debate whether all the movements we ask from our horses are "natural."

realizes he's not trapped, and he quits doing the natural thing — trying to run.

Another natural, but ineffective, line of thinking is to speed up our request when we want the horse to respond more quickly. When we are waiting for the horse to respond, we naturally think that if we put more energy into our request, he'll put more energy into his response. But it doesn't work that way. **If we want a faster response, we should slow our cues, giving the horse time to respond before things get intense. He learns that if he responds right away, he'll save himself extra aggravation.** But, if he figures out that you aren't going to give him time to respond, he'll give up and become sluggish in responding.

Think for a moment about what our instinctive reaction is when there's a wreck going on — say, a horse exploding in a trailer. We want to rush in to "help." But, when we help, the wreck usually gets bigger. In many cases it only makes the horse panic more, and it puts both us and the horse in danger. We have to train ourselves to stand back, wait for all the noise to quit, then sneak up and look into the trailer to see if there's anything left worth getting out. That's not natural to do, but we have to learn to do it.

Giving to the bit

It is no more natural for the horse to "give to the bit" than for us to correctly ask him to give. When we take all the slack out of the rein, every horse will pull on the rein, trying to get us to let go. Every rider naturally lets the horse move their hand, and in doing so, sends a signal to the horse that if he pulls hard enough, he can get the rein to move. It takes major concentration to do the unnatural — to lock your hand down against that saddle and wait for the horse to "give." (Come to mention it, waiting for anything doesn't come naturally.)

Natural — good or bad?

We could go on and on, about how it's not natural to keep horses in a barn, to drive them around in trailers, to feed them baled hay instead of letting them graze and so forth. Does that mean that unnatural is bad?

No, in fact, by separating horses instead of letting them all live together in one pasture, we prevent major injuries. By putting shoes on their feet, we keep them from tearing up their hooves. By blanketing our old horse, we make his life much more comfortable. And by using wisdom in knowing when natural is helpful or when the unnatural is better, we can significantly improve our horse's lot in life.

That's really the major point of this discussion. We really do our horses and ourselves a disservice if we let "natural" be the guideline for what is right to do. Take this scenario, for example.

You are peacefully walking along out on the trail, and a dog jumps out of the bushes. Your horse spooks, which is natural. You snatch the reins, which is natural. He gets more excited and scared, raises his head and prepares to escape, which is natural — you get the idea. You can say, "Well, John. That's too obvious that natural reactions can get us into trouble. We wouldn't do that."

Well, let's change the situation. You are trying to lead your horse down the driveway, and he's diving for grass, which is natural. **It's also natural for you to pull on the lead rope when he pulls his head down.** Because he's stronger, you get frustrated and jerk the rope, which is natural, and get mad at the horse for not obeying you. That would be a natural reaction. But, is it reasonable for a horse to do what you want him to do, when you are venting your frustration, instead of giving him a cue? Of course not.

So, instead of our doing what comes naturally when our horse does what comes naturally to him, we should ask ourselves:
1) Is what he's doing natural?
2) What do I wish he was doing?
3) What is my cue to tell him to do what I want him to do?

React or respond?

So, what is a natural reaction to reading a chapter like this? To agree that natural isn't always best, recall some natural behavior of a fellow horseman, then presume that because we have absorbed this lesson intellectually, our behavior is going to follow suit. **It's natural for us to expect performance without practice — but that doesn't work.**

So, what unnatural thing do I recommend? Brainstorm about what behavior you'd like to see changed in your horse (or yourself/kids, etc.). We'll call that Point A. Determine what behavior you are going to replace it with (Point Z). Then develop a step-by-step lesson plan to get from Point A to Z. Before long, you'll be enjoying your horse's good performance, as you listen to other riders give a hundred "natural" excuses why their horse is out of control. ■PH

A natural reaction or a trained response?

Behavior: Pulls his head away when I bridle him.
Is it natural? Yes
What trained response would I prefer?
   Drop his head. Open his mouth on cue.
What cues should I teach?
   Head down cue. Open mouth cue.

Behavior: Runs into me and steps on my feet when I lead him.
Is it natural? Yes
What trained response would I prefer?
   Respect my space.
   Move his shoulders away from me when I tell him.
   Walk forward without pulling on me, etc.
What cues should I teach?
   Leading lessons. Go forward cue.
   WESN lesson. Control that hip lesson.

Behavior: Panics when he's left behind on the trail.
Is it natural? Yes
What trained response would I prefer?
   Pay attention to me. Calm down.
What cues should I teach?
   Calm down cue. Give to the bit. Speed control.

Behavior: Rears when he doesn't want to leave the barn area.
Is it natural? Yes
What trained response would I prefer?
   Head at normal height. Go forward to my leg cue.
What cues should I teach?
   Rear-ending lesson. Speed control. Buddy sour.

Behavior: Visits every horse as I lead him down the barn aisle.
Is it natural? Yes
What trained response would I prefer?
   Good halter manners.
What cues should I teach?
   Hip control. Yield to pressure. Give to the bit.

Notes

18

Evaluating A Clinic

When we go to a clinic or demonstration,
we want timely, usable information.
But how do we know if what we see there is something
we should take home and try with our own horse?

At demonstrations, I often ask how many people would like
to have a horse as well trained as Zip. Lots of hands go
up. Then I ask how many would like a horse better trained
than Zip. I get puzzled looks. Then I ask, would you like
to find ways to teach your horse easier than I did Zip? People are
dumbfounded. They look at Zip as a well-trained horse, which
he is, but that's not to say that someone else couldn't train their
horse better and easier than I did Zip. And, since there are no real
"secrets" to good horse training, why shouldn't someone else benefit from what I've discovered? That's the whole idea behind going
to clinics — learn what someone else does, and add it to your own
base of knowledge.

When you watch a clinic you should go home having learned
about horses and a particular training method. You should either be
eager to put what you've seen into practice or have recognized what
not to do. We'll give you some guidelines for evaluating a clinic or
demonstration and a checklist to take with you so you can get the
most out of your clinic dollars.

We'll suggest questions that could sound either positive or negative, depending on your mindset. For instance, "Does the situation appear safe?" One person might look for safety features, like
good footing, while another might only spot the potential dangers.
I recommend a balanced approach that recognizes both. It's easy to
sit in the stands and criticize, but that isn't the objective.

Clinic evaluation checklist

Date: _____ *Clinician:* _____

My reason for attending:

_____

_____

Safety:
■ *Are the horse's legs reasonably protected?*
■ *Is the fencing secure and without sharp edges?*
■ *Does the training appear safe for the horse and trainer?*

Trainer/Clinician:
■ *Does the trainer genuinely seem to like the horse?*
Is he patient, with both the horse and questions from onlookers?
■ *Does he talk mostly about horses and horse training, or about himself?*
■ *Is the clinician a learner, or does he have a "copy-only-me" attitude?*
■ *Does the trainer seem more interested in doing what's best for the demonstration horse or in putting on a good show?*
■ *How many wrecks or fights did he have with the horse, and how did he handle them?*
■ *When correction was used, did it seem right? Did it create unwanted side effects? Was there anger in the clinician's hands?*

Education:
■ *Does the trainer thoroughly explain what he's doing and why?*
■ *Does he make the horse look good, like a willing student?*
■ *Do I understand the steps involved in the training?*

My Instinct:
■ *What is my overall feeling about the training?*
■ *Would I feel good about my horse being the demonstration horse?*

Why are you going to the clinic?

Is it to learn training specifics or general concepts, or is it really for entertainment? There's nothing wrong with any of those answers. But, if I went to a Barbra Streisand concert, for instance, although I'd have a great evening, I wouldn't come home a better singer. On the other hand, even though you may be going for entertainment's sake, you can still learn. You don't have to walk away from every demonstration ready to do what the trainer did.

Assuming you plan to put new knowledge to use, look for how you might duplicate what the trainer is doing. **It's unlikely that the clinician/trainer will do things the way you do them — that doesn't mean either of you is "right" or "wrong."**

TWO KINDS OF CLINICIANS THAT FREQUENTLY SHOW UP ON THE CLINIC CIRCUIT ARE THE GUY WHO CAN'T RIDE A BUCKING HORSE AND THE GUY WHO LOVES TO RIDE BUCKING HORSES.

Staying safe

Evaluate everything from a safety perspective. The No. 1 and No. 2 rules that I use to evaluate any type of training are: "The trainer can't get hurt," and "the horse can't get hurt." Training a horse is never worth getting injured. So keep safety in mind as you watch. That includes checking to see if the horse has leg protection if he needs it, and that the working area is safe. It means watching what goes on both in and outside the arena. During the training, watch to see if the trainer gives the horse a chance to catch his breath, or if he seems to work him too hard.

Safety also applies to any type of restraint or bits — is the equipment safe? If the horse fights, can he get injured? How you would feel if that were your horse being worked in the demonstration?

Ideally, a clinician should be able to demonstrate what he or she is teaching.

Teacher and student

Next, I would look at the trainer. Obviously there is an entertainment factor in good teaching — no instructor wants to bore the audience, so nearly everyone tries to liven things up by cracking a joke now and then. But, who gets the brunt of the jokes? Does the trainer repeatedly make fun of the horse, an owner or other trainers? If so, though his jokes may seem funny, no one learns much by being put down. That's because a teacher has to respect his pupils — both horse and human — in order to teach them well.

If the trainer builds up the horse or the audience, that's helpful. If he gives you the sense that you could do that, too, he builds confidence for both the horse and audience. But, if he's sarcastic or talks down to the participants — either horses or people — he'll end up discouraging them. He may not intend to, and, in fact, it may be just a style of teaching that he's adopted, but the effect is the same as if he really thought them incapable of progress.

Does the trainer seem to like the horse? Do you notice him stroking the horse, or does he slap him hard to tell him that he's done a good job? What kind of equipment is the trainer using, and does he use it kindly?

Does the horse have a chance to respond to the trainer's requests before the trainer corrects him? And, how does the trainer or his associates handle the horse outside the demonstration area? These are matters that reflect whether the student can have confidence in his teacher.

What would you say about the trainer's attitude? Does he remind you of your favorite grade-school teacher? Is this a person who would listen if you asked a question that someone else might think is "stupid" or overly complicated? If not, his patience with the horse may be limited, too. Since the right answer is always clearer to the teacher than the student, the teacher must be always patient. (If the student already knew the answer, he wouldn't need a teacher.) **We have to assume that horses learn at the kindergarten level or below,** so that tells you something about the kind of teacher a horse needs.

Is the clinician a learner, or does he have a "copy-only-me" attitude? Is he basically telling you that he's a "guru" — that he has the definitive word on horse training? If so, then he's also telling you that his mind is closed to further learning — and that his mind closed long ago, on the day he decided he knew all the answers. Does the guy talk more about himself than about horse training? If so, you know what you are learning about.

Does the trainer speak well of other trainers or riders, or does he play a one-upsmanship game, doing one better than people around him or other trainers? If the former, you'll find yourself looking for the good in other people's teaching, also. But, if the latter, he's concerned with himself, and not teaching you or your horse.

We all know that good horse training is really common sense. **So, does the training make sense**, or does the trainer make it so complicated that it seems like rocket science, or worse yet, make it look easy but sound too complicated for you to duplicate?

Equipment doesn't train a horse — good training principles do. Does the trainer rely on special equipment or on training principles?

Does he explain why he trains as he does or **is his training proprietary** — implying that unless you use his training system or equipment, you'll be ineffective with your horse?

Does the trainer lead you to think there are great secrets in his method? Do his followers seem eager to be of genuine help to you or just want to tell you how great their hero is?

The trainer's performance

All clinicians, particularly if they are from "somewhere else," are 1) under pressure to perform, and 2) probably on their best behavior.

It's always good to inject a little tasteful humor into a training session, both when training privately and in front of a crowd.

Is the trainer making realistic demands on the horse, or is he skipping big steps in the training process? If he depends on his years of experience or talent, rather than the steps in the training, you'll have a hard time duplicating his technique.

There are many kinds of clinicians. Two that frequently show up on the clinic circuit are the guy who can't ride a bucking horse and the guy who loves to ride bucking horses. For any number of reasons, a trainer may have another person get into the saddle instead of himself. That's OK, but watch what he does carefully and **evaluate if you think you'd be ready to step into the saddle when the rider does**. If not, there may have been some steps missed in the training.

Then there's the guy born to conquer territory. In fact, it makes him look like a really good rider if the horse bucks when he first gets on. If you follow his training, you may end up on a bucking horse, too.

Good training should make the training technique look easy. It often looks like nothing much is happening in the ring, because often what's happening is going on inside of the horse's head and emotions. Horses need time to have emotions go up and down, like people do. And, unless you have a friend you are willing to sacrifice on your bucking horse or just like the thrill of the ride, you don't want to see too much activity in your training ring either.

Regardless of what type of correction the trainer uses, is he consistent? Does the horse know what behavior is being corrected? Does the horse have a chance to get it right the next time? If the trainer is acting in anger, the correction will be sporadic — too much at one time and too little at another. **Different training systems use different means of correction, but no correction should be done out of the trainer's frustration or aggravation.** And, because no horse ever intentionally does anything to make someone look stupid, if the trainer is acting in a stupid way, he's responsible for his own behavior — no horse made him do anything.

BOTTOM LINE: WOULD YOU FEEL GOOD ABOUT YOUR HORSE BEING IN THE DEMONSTRATION RING?

The demonstration horse

Does the demonstration horse look like a winner or a loser? Winners get taught, losers get thumped on. **A horse doesn't excel, any more than a person does, by getting told all the stuff he does wrong.** But, if there are enough steps in the training that the horse can go from one success to the next, he'll be a star in no time.

Does the horse look easy or hard to train? Better trainers make the horse look easy. Poor trainers try to make the horse look bad, so they can look good. The less knowledge a trainer has, the more his "show" may depend on the horse looking bad. Everyone runs across a difficult horse or an easy horse, so this isn't the sole criteria. Do you remember the movie, "To Sir, With Love" (I may be really dating myself here)? The kids in a classroom were really unruly with one teacher, but the other teacher made the same kids look good.

Trainers can pick a fight just so they look like they are doing something out there, and in fact they are — but it's not necessarily good training. **For training to build correctly, look for areas where the trainer and the horse get along, not argue.**

Is the horse getting more calm as the lesson proceeds, or does the horse seem to be getting increasingly aggravated, even though he may be performing seemingly correctly? **Rule No. 3 that I use in evaluating any training method is: "Is the horse calmer at the end of the lesson than at the beginning?"** Scared horses don't learn any better than scared kids do. Both need a sense of security — that they're OK and can do what's being asked of them — in order for them to progress in their education.

Don't join the crowd

Watching a horse-training demonstration, there are usually a lot of people who think highly of the clinician, a few sharp-tongued critics and some folks there to learn. Ignore what people are saying around you — usually the ones who are talking know the least. The ones who are there to learn do the least talking.

Ignore what people tell you about other trainers. More wrong information about this one or that one's training gets passed around at other trainers' clinics than anywhere else. Again, it's not usually people in the know who are doing the talking. It's people who saw part of someone else's tape, or who heard a story passed along to them. **Because the industry is so guru-oriented, folks often think**

The same "rules of engagement" should apply when training alone as when teaching a clinic.

that talking one trainer down makes another one look good, but putting someone else down is never constructive.

By the way, I'm frequently asked what I think of this or that trainer. I rarely comment. Usually when I'm asked about what I think about how so-and-so deals with, for instance, a horse who bites, I tell them that it isn't for me to evaluate another training method for them. I tell them my solution to a horse who bites, and then they have to determine what will work in their situation.

The way we do it at home

No one paying money to watch a trainer really cares how you do it at home — or that you've watched this same trainer in 47 clinics. **Since you'll be going to the demonstration with the attitude of a learner, be considerate of the people around you and don't distract them from the exhibition with tales from back at your ranch.** People can't listen to you and watch a demonstration. Besides, you can't talk and learn what's going on in the ring at the same time. Don't cheat someone else or yourself out of a learning experience.

A few questions to ask yourself: Do I know so much that I can't learn anymore? Am I attending the clinic so I can learn, or so I feel important or can say that I've been to watch so-and-so? When I watch, do I look for the first thing that I disagree with, so I can come home feeling pumped up about myself or down on the know-nothing trainer in the ring? Am I really looking to justify some type of training that I do, or am I there to see how I can expand my knowledge? Pretty straight stuff — but there's no sense evaluating the clinician if you're not willing to take the same test.

The content of the course

While you're watching the trainer, does what he's doing seem to be sequential? Can you determine what the objective of each exercise is, or, better yet, does the clinician explain what he's doing? Does the horse's activity match the trainer's explanation? Sometimes a horse really isn't doing what the trainer wants, but, because there's a crowd watching, there's also pressure to make it sound good. That's OK for the show, but it won't help you at home.

Remember back at the beginning of this chapter, we asked why you were going to the demonstration? Depending on your answer, you'll want to know a few specifics. For instance, if you plan to use the demonstrated technique with your own horse, do you understand the concept well enough that you can fill in the blanks yourself, or do you really need step-by-step instructions? **If you need additional help, where can you get it? That's a valid question to ask the trainer if there's a question-and-answer session. Since so much of horse training is finding out what not to do, you might ask him what difficulties a person might run into if they tried to do what he demonstrated.**

Then, too, watch carefully to see if the lesson or correction used creates unwanted behaviors. For instance, it doesn't matter how great the trainer has the horse changing leads if his neck is stiff and his tail swishes every time, or if he has a beautiful headset but is getting progressively headshy.

Putting it to work for you

Trust your instincts. After "objective" evaluation, you'll have a gut feeling about the training. Bottom line: Would you feel good about your horse being in the demonstration ring? **You'll likely pattern what you do after what you've seen, whether you think highly of it or not, so consciously decide what part you want to duplicate.**

After all is said and done, incorporate what you've found valuable with what you already know. No one knows it all — not you or me or the clinician in the ring. If I thought that I had all the horse-training answers, I'd be a fool. I really work at watching how horses respond to other riders, and I listen to other trainers when I can. But, I don't just copy them — I rely on my own judgment and use the best of what I've learned.

Let me give you an analogy. If I wanted to be as good a photographer as Ansel Adams, I could find the exact locations where he took his photos, use just the right film and equipment, and wait until the light was right, then snap a photo. I might even be able to hang my Ansel Adams look-alike alongside his original. But I'd never be able to do anything better than that.

On the other hand, if I studied what Ansel Adams did, and added that to what I already knew and what I could learn from other photographers, I might end up a better photographer than Adams.

My training is constantly changing — a product of the fact that I'm always learning. None of us knows how good a trainer we'll be tomorrow. We have to work at it today and learn from everyone that we can. Sometimes we learn what to do and sometimes what not to do. But the key is to adopt the attitude of a learner, whether you teach for a living or not. ■

19

Keeping It Positive

Equestrian coach and competitor Barbra Schulte points to a link between mind, body and emotion — and shows you how it may radically change your riding and training efforts.

A s your horse's trainer, caretaker and rider, you represent at least 50 percent of the equation, horse + person = team. It's a big responsibility that often comes with a load of stresses along with the joy. So, how can you make sure the pressures don't overshadow the pleasures, and the stresses don't cloud your senses?

Part of the answer lies in gaining an awareness of the connections between your mind, your body and your emotions, and in learning how to control each to create a positive effect on your whole person — according to Barbra Schulte, champion cutting horse trainer and the only certified equestrian coach for the Mentally Tough Training program. Communication with cues is more than learning what signals to give our horses. It's also training ourselves — teaching ourselves cues and conditioning ourselves to respond to them. Barbra Schulte tells us how.

The daughter of legendary cutting horse trainer Cletus Hulling, Barbra Schulte grew up riding and, in 1992, became the first woman to win the NCHA Derby and Superstakes.

Barbra Schulte trains and competes, along with teaching cutting and Mentally Tough Training.

Perfect Horse: *What is Mentally Tough Training?*

Barbra Schulte: Mentally Tough is a system used by top athletes in all major sports. It teaches students to integrate their mental, physical and emotional actions (and reactions) to achieve their highest potential under even the most stressful conditions.

PH: *Before this interview, you told us that Mentally Tough Training helped you even today.*

Schulte: Yes. Three yearlings came down with an infection last week. Two of them — a colt and a filly, which were owned by other people — seemed to be responding great to treatment. The other filly belongs to my husband and me, and she was in bad shape. She had to have a tracheotomy, and she lost a lot of weight. The vet came out and said repeatedly that the other two appeared to be out of the woods, so I left for a trip today.

When I called home, I learned that the filly we didn't own had died, and the other two yearlings were doing worse.

My first response was guilt. Yet I had been there, working with the vet every day, doing everything I could. So I just kept saying to myself, "What do I have control over?" I had no control over the death of that filly. I had to let it go.

That's a basic principle of Mentally Tough, distinguishing which events you can control and which you cannot, and learning not to dwell on things you have no control over.

PH: *Tell us more.*

Schulte: Today's situation touches on the need to develop life skills, one of which is recovery: When you have traumas in life, you have to have recovery. You teach yourself to recover energy and to relax on demand. Recovery can be anything that helps you relieve stress, from getting enough sleep, proper nutrition and sufficient exercise to spending time with family and friends, reading and enjoying leisure-time activities.

In my case, I got to the airport for my trip and wanted to make some changes in my travel plans. I was told that would cost $1,000. Then I was late for this interview. And I was dealing with the filly's death and having to tell the owner. I gave myself about 15 minutes to try to get focused so I could talk with you. If I'd pushed through it instead of giving myself recovery time, I wouldn't have been able to give you a good interview.

You have to learn to recognize the need for recovery, to know when you are stressed and to give yourself time to relax. After we finish talking and I get on the plane, I will allow myself to relax, rather than working on some speaking projects.

That part of the Mentally Tough Training has been one of the most dramatically positive influences in my life. I used to push and push, but now I realize I need enough sleep and the right diet and enough recovery time in order to perform to my maximum ability. If I take even a few minutes of recovery, it refreshes me.

Toughness training profile

This is a profile riders use to evaluate their mental toughness. It refers to actions and attitudes at a time under pressure, such as before a competition or on a trail ride, not traits in general. All of the areas represent trained or changeable/attainable patterns of thinking and behaving.

- *The higher scores represent areas of strength.*

• *The lower scores represent areas of weakness. Riders should note the four lowest scores and develop mental images and/or "scripts" to help develop stronger patterns of thinking and acting to strengthen these areas.*

For each attribute, circle the number, on the scale of 1 to 10 that best represents how you see yourself under pressure. You may want to ask several people who know you well to fill it out, indicating how they see you respond under pressure. That will help you determine if you are perceived by others the same way you see yourself.

Anxious	1·2·3·4·5·6·7·8·9·10	Calm
Unfocused	1·2·3·4·5·6·7·8·9·10	Focused
Impatient	1·2·3·4·5·6·7·8·9·10	Patient
External	1·2·3·4·5·6·7·8·9·10	Instinctive
Pessimistic	1·2·3·4·5·6·7·8·9·10	Optimistic
Low energy	1·2·3·4·5·6·7·8·9·10	Energized
Emotionally rigid	1·2·3·4·5·6·7·8·9·10	Emotionally flexible
Irresponsible	1·2·3·4·5·6·7·8·9·10	Responsible
Non-responsive	1·2·3·4·5·6·7·8·9·10	Responsive
Non-resilient	1·2·3·4·5·6·7·8·9·10	Resilient
Tense	1·2·3·4·5·6·7·8·9·10	Relaxed
Fearful	1·2·3·4·5·6·7·8·9·10	Challenged
Moody	1·2·3·4·5·6·7·8·9·10	Even tempered
Dependent	1·2·3·4·5·6·7·8·9·10	Self-reliant
Undisciplined	1·2·3·4·5·6·7·8·9·10	Disciplined
Passive	1·2·3·4·5·6·7·8·9·10	Assertive
Uncommitted	1·2·3·4·5·6·7·8·9·10	Committed
Insecure	1·2·3·4·5·6·7·8·9·10	Confident
Uncoachable	1·2·3·4·5·6·7·8·9·10	Coachable
Poor sense of humor	1·2·3·4·5·6·7·8·9·10	Great sense of humor
Unmotivated	1·2·3·4·5·6·7·8·9·10	Motivated
Physically unfit	1·2·3·4·5·6·7·8·9·10	Physically fit
Poor problem solver	1·2·3·4·5·6·7·8·9·10	Good problem solver
Defensive	1·2·3·4·5·6·7·8·9·10	Open
Unwilling to take risks	1·2·3·4·5·6·7·8·9·10	Willing to take risks
Not playful	1·2·3·4·5·6·7·8·9·10	Playful/fun loving
Unskilled at acting	1·2·3·4·5·6·7·8·9·10	Skilled at acting
Negative body language	1·2·3·4·5·6·7·8·9·10	Positive body language
Unfriendly	1·2·3·4·5·6·7·8·9·10	Friendly
Not open to change	1·2·3·4·5·6·7·8·9·10	Open to change

Copyright© LGE Sports Science, Inc. 1996

PH: *Is Mentally Tough Training about relieving stress?*

Schulte: It's more than that. Mentally Tough Training teaches you to achieve and control your Ideal Performance State, which is a combination of high positive emotions that most people are familiar with as being "on" or "in the zone." Using Mentally Tough Training you learn how to summon that state any time, any place, under any circumstances. And the training encompasses all aspects of your life.

PH: *Can you give us some examples of what the Mentally Tough Training process involves?*

Schulte: Sure. You learn to train your emotions by using your mind and your body. For instance, scripting is one of the main mind skills you learn. This is basically talking to yourself, but with a purpose. You learn to talk to yourself in ways that keep you focused and positive, so that you are filling your head with technical instruction — like notes to yourself on following John's training techniques — as well as positive thoughts.

Most of us coach ourselves about what we don't want to do. For instance, if your horse shies at logs when you trail ride, the tendency is to tell yourself, "I hope my horse doesn't balk at the logs today." This actually promotes a negative emotional response when you get near the log, which leads to a negative physical response — your muscles get tense, your breathing becomes shallow, your heart rate increases. And your horse shies at the log.

A change of script to a positive statement reflects what you want to happen. For instance, you might say, "The logs on the trail will be a great challenge. I know that by asking for my horse's attention before we reach the logs, my horse will do the right thing, and I will feel great."

By creating this different visual set in your mind, you give yourself a whole new emotional response to the situation, so that your mind and body do not follow that negative path. You stay relaxed and focused on the positive and give yourself a scenario for accomplishing what you want to achieve. And when you realize you have control over your response to the situation, it empowers you and you have fun.

PH: *How does it work?*

Schulte: Your emotions and your mental state affect you physically. When you feel tired, lethargic, wired or frustrated, your muscles tighten, you lose balance and coordination, and you don't think clearly. It works in reverse, too: The physical conditions can trigger an emotional response. This can work in your favor, because you can trigger positive emotion by using positive physical posturing. For instance, by keeping your chin up, eyes held in the direction you're headed, shoulders back and breathing rhythmically, you will gain a feeling of confidence.

PH: *How does Mentally Tough Training apply to the recreational or non-competitive rider?*

Schulte: Competitor or not, we all have the desire to achieve our goals and reach the highest level we can. The reason we ride is for the connection with the horse and the pure pleasure of it. Our horses give us a way to stretch ourselves and to grow in an area that is challenging and interesting to us.

The difference between a competitor and a leisure rider is that the competitor chooses to "test" his or her skills in a pressure situation where the results are compared to other riders. Leisure riders may not be in competition, but that doesn't mean they don't face high-stress pressure situations, even in trail riding. Maintaining a calm physiological state in an emergency situation gives them the best potential to respond appropriately, and they do this by reaching their Ideal Performance State.

PH: *How does our Ideal Performance State affect our horses?*

Schulte: Our emotions trigger physiological responses in ourselves that also seem to be connected to our horses' emotions, as if an electrical current were transferring our feelings directly to our horse.

So let's say you're working with your horse, but things aren't going the way you want them to. You start getting frustrated and you lose emotional control. At that point, there's no way you can think clearly. Your brain-wave patterns are disrupted, your heart rate increases, and your overall potential to stay focused and communicate with your horse is impaired.

But when you maintain your Ideal Performance State your heart rate slows, your brain pattern becomes rhythmic, you relax, and you are able to focus and think clearly.

PH: *What made you turn to Mentally Tough Training?*

Schulte: For 10 years, I was a traditional cutting horse trainer with

30 to 40 horses in the barn. I was on the road two weeks or more out of every month. I found that I couldn't connect as well with the people or the horses. So I asked myself, "What makes riding fun for me?" Then I arranged my life so that I could pursue what it was that made riding fun.

That's the most important thing: Keep it fun. If you're in a situation that's not fun, no one else is responsible for changing that except yourself. That may sound harsh, but the bottom line is you need to create as much fun as you can in the time you have. Be on your own program and don't compare it to other people's.

Right now, I strive for excellence in my horses and to enjoy the competition. I've taken away the pressure to win. It's important for everyone to evaluate what riding means to them — that's part of visualizing the future. You have to keep asking yourself, "What makes it good for me?" PH

Thoughts for today

Help yourself maintain a positive outlook by creating a mindset to follow. For example, you might tell yourself:

1. Just for today, I will find humor in my mistakes. When I can smile inside, I am in control.

2. Just for today, I will have a plan to follow. The plan will keep me focused and organized.

3. Just for today, I will set aside some time to relax and simply let go. Relaxation is an essential part of training.

4. Just for today, I will do the best I can. I will be satisfied with what I have done.

5. Just for today, I will do the ordinary things in my training extraordinarily well. It's the little things that make the difference.

From James E. Loehr, Ed.D., founder of LGE Sport Science, Inc. and creator of Mentally Tough Training.
Barbra Schulte/Center for Equestrian Performance 800-737-1070/409-277-9344

Notes

20

Hallelujah!

Despite Lou's years of headshyness and pulling back, Hatsie taught her old mare new Lyons' tricks.

ou is headshy, no doubt about it. Hallelujah, "Lou" for short, is a 15-year-old Connemara Thoroughbred who had a rough beginning in life — and remembers it. Hatsie has owned her for the last 12 years, and together they've worked through lots of things, but not headshyness. Though Lou doesn't react violently to everything, Hatsie is careful about tying her anywhere she might get upset, and she is forced to use scissors to cut a bridlepath. Yet even that can be dangerous. She is able to bridle the horse, but only if she is very gentle and careful about Lou's ears, so Hatsie has been sweet-talking her and gently sneaking the bridle on her for a long time.

Lou is a good performance mare. Because she is obedient and does her job well, Hatsie tries not to bother her with "unimportant" things. Hatsie loves Lou and would enjoy showing

Hallelujah took the threat of being clipped seriously, causing herself pain and endangering Hatsie.

her affection, but Lou is aloof, preferring not to have too much attention or handling, as if she's saying, "Give me my assignment and leave me alone." **Hatsie is sure that beneath that exterior toughness is a fearful horse waiting to be set free.** As there is no round pen available, Hatsie set out to work with what she had. She wanted to develop a program she could use on the days she had only a few minutes to work with her horses.

The plan

Hatsie reviewed the training principles before developing a lesson plan. First, she was determined not to put herself in a position to get hurt, which, as you can see by the photos, was a real possibility if Lou felt pressured. Second, she certainly wasn't going to let Lou get hurt after all these years of babying her. And third, Lou needed to be calmer at the end of the lesson than at the beginning.

First, Hatsie wanted to teach Lou a cue to drop her head. **Her goal was to put her hand on Lou's poll (top of her head, between the ears) and have the horse bring her head down.** Well, there was no touching the top of her head, and "down" was not where Lou intended her head to go. As you can imagine, if Hatsie were to have pulled down on the lead rope, Lou's head would have gone up farther. In fact, sometimes Lou's feet went up as well as her head. Hatsie needed a system that would let her get to Lou's head.

Hatsie put Lou's halter and lead rope on her, and led her outside the barn area. (Lou is more defensive in the barn than outside.) She decided to do this exercise without tying her because tying Lou is

Lou pulled her head away, expecting Hatsie to put pressure on the lead rope, but Hatsie continued to keep contact with Lou's neck.

dangerous, so tying would have violated John's training rules No. 1 and No. 2. Hatsie petted Lou's shoulder one stroke, then turned away. A moment later, she turned back to Lou, stroked her shoulder again, and again turned away. Six times she did this.

The seventh time, she stroked her neck just in front of the withers and turned away again, as before. Hatsie repeated this stroking and turning away another four times, then stroked twice before turning away. She continued stroking and turning away until she worked her way up to stroking just behind the poll.

She took her time, each stroke now lasting a few seconds. **If she thought Lou might pull away in four seconds, she stayed with her for only three.** Sometimes she guessed wrong, and Lou moved her head away before Hatsie could withdraw her hand. Of course, Hatsie did not want Lou to think that she could escape her contact by pulling away, as she'd done thousands of times in the past. So, when Lou pulled away, Hatsie didn't put pressure on the lead rope, as she'd always done before; instead, let the lead rope stay slack, but her right hand followed Lou's neck until her neck muscles softened. Then Hatsie withdrew her hand.

In stepping away from Lou, Hatsie ended one training segment, beginning a new one seconds later. By now, she could see Lou beginning to understand that an agreement was forming. Hatsie was not going to overpower her or trap her for endless periods. Lou's posture began to send the message that instead of reacting first and thinking later (as defensive horses do), she would wait a moment to see what was happening.

Little by little, Lou allowed Hatsie to stroke her for longer periods without pulling away. The expression in her eye softened and she looked less defensive, yet Hatsie could sense that if she pressured her or grabbed the halter, Lou would pull away in a heartbeat.

Eventually, Lou could stand quietly for Hatsie to put her hand on her poll for a moment before withdrawing. All of this was to reach a starting point for teaching the "head down" cue.

Asking for her head to drop

By now, Lou was tolerating Hatsie's hand on her poll, for a moment at least. The new objective was to have Lou drop her head when Hatsie rested her hand on Lou's poll. With Lou standing relatively relaxed, Hatsie rested her hand on top of Lou's head. After about three seconds, Lou was ready for Hatsie to remove her hand. Lou tensed her neck, but Hatsie remained calm, keeping her hand on Lou's poll.

When Lou raised her head an inch or two, Hatsie just went along with her. Even though Lou is pretty tall and Hatsie's hand slid down the neck just a little, the effect was the same as keeping her hand on the poll. As the pressure on her poll did not increase and Hatsie was not going away, Lou relaxed her neck enough to let her head drop about a half inch. Hatsie removed her hand and turned away from Lou, as she had done in the exercise just minutes before.

Hatsie then turned back to Lou and, talking with her softly, petted her neck a few times before resting her hand again on Lou's poll. (By now, Hatsie's day was already a success, you realize, even if nothing more was accomplished.) Lou again raised her head after four seconds, and again Hatsie went along with her. When Lou dropped her head about a half inch, Hatsie withdrew her hand.

UNTIL NOW, CLIPPING LOU'S EARS
HAS BEEN OUT OF THE QUESTION. MY
ONLY CONSOLATION WAS THAT HER EARS
WEREN'T TOO FURRY, AND I COULD GET
AWAY WITH SHOWING HER WITH
THEM UNCLIPPED.

It was now much easier to pet Lou's neck and reach up to her poll. Hatsie repeated the process five or six times, each time Lou raising her head less than the time before. Eventually she wasn't raising her head at all, but after four or five seconds, started to drop her head. **As soon as Hatsie felt downward movement, she withdrew her hand.**

Hatsie must have petted Lou a couple of hundred times by now, and Lou was going along with the program pretty well. In fact, it seemed that she was going to sleep. Not only did her eyes half close, but when Hatsie put her hand on Lou's poll, Lou didn't move at all. But Hatsie was committed for the long haul and was not about to stop now. If all Hatsie had wanted to do was desensitize Lou to her hand on the poll, she'd have reached her goal. Her goal was not de-sensitization, but response to a cue. **The cue was her hand resting on Lou's poll; the response she wanted to get every time was for**

Hatsie felt successful, just being able to reach Lou's head and not have her pull away.

Hatsie withdrew her hand and turned away from Lou's head each time, ending that training segment.

Lou to drop her head. Now Hatsie could rest her hand on Lou's poll (in effect, giving her the cue), but nothing was happening.

So, she waited while Lou appeared to sleep. Seconds passed, which felt like minutes after Hatsie had spent nearly an hour extending her arm. Lou dropped her head. Hatsie withdrew her hand and told Lou what a good girl she was. She petted her shoulder and once more rested her hand on Lou's head. With little hesitation, Lou's head went down. Again Hatsie withdrew her hand and petted Lou. Again she rested her hand on Lou's head, but this time nothing happened. She waited. When she thought the head moved down a smidge, she removed her hand. Again and again, when Lou's head seemed to move downward at Hatsie's request, Hatsie gave her the benefit of the doubt. Hatsie walked Lou a step or two, not sure if the mare was falling asleep or just losing concentration.

A moment later when she rested her hand on Lou's poll, the head went down instantly, and about six inches — a breakthrough! By comparison, each movement downward until now had seemed grudging. Hatsie stroked Lou's mane a couple of times then rested her hand on her poll. After four seconds, Lou dropped her head about six inches. It seemed that Lou knew what Hatsie was asking and that she was willing to cooperate. Over and over, each time her head got lower, Hatsie withdrew her hand, petted her shoulder or turned away.

Finally, Hatsie was able to reach around Lou's neck to give her a big hug. This was impressive, and very rewarding to Hatsie, who has loved this mare for many years. Lou stayed relaxed and even seemed to enjoy the attention. Hallelujah!

Hatsie's comments

Long ago, I tried sedating Lou, which didn't work at all because she broke through the drugs. She'd be standing droop-eared and I'd begin to pull her mane or approach her ears, and she'd spring into action. Recently, I tried tying her so that she couldn't get away, hoping that she would teach herself the futility of overreacting. She didn't learn anything, and it was traumatic for both of us.

Until now, clipping her ears has been out of the question. My only consolation was that her ears weren't too furry, and I could get away with showing her with them unclipped.

I was doubtful of any turnaround and was delighted to see her go from being fearful to being more trusting. In the days since this first lesson, she has been easier to catch in the field, and she puts her head down readily when I work with her outside. She is still pretty tense in the barn but is getting better. I'm eager to continue to work with this system, perhaps with the hose next, as she won't let me wash her neck or head, then on to sacking her out and teaching her to stand tied. **PH**

21

Catch Him First

You can't begin training a horse
until you can catch him — or can you?
This real-life story is about Donna and Markiz.

Donna works full time and dreams of showing her horses, but time, circumstances and their level of training stand between Donna and her goal. Her Arabians, Odessa, a chestnut mare, and Markiz, a bay gelding, live in an 11-acre pasture, seven of which are a pond. The wire fencing is relatively secure for ordinary pasture life, but you wouldn't want the horses to challenge it. There is no round pen or corral nearby, and Markiz' history of trailering problems makes taking him to a training barn unrealistic.

Markiz is a friendly horse, on his terms, but afraid of everything. He is headshy, bucks when ridden, and spooks badly over seemingly nothing. He has been to professional trainers who find him a chore to ride, and, because of his spookiness, Donna is afraid to ride him.

But riding isn't the first problem she's tackling; catching him is. Once he's caught and tied, Donna can groom him, but getting him caught is a challenge. She decided one Saturday that this was the day to work with him. He was wearing the fly mask he'd been wearing for days. While she'd prefer he didn't wear a fly mask for a training session, he was used to wearing it and catching him to take it off would have been a problem.

Donna reviewed John's principles about not getting hurt and the horse not getting hurt and the horse being calmer at the end of the lesson. Then the rule, **"Go to a point in the training where you can ask the horse to do something and have him do it consistently."**

The plan

There really wasn't anything Donna could ask Markiz to do and have him do it consistently, although she could get him to tolerate things if he was restrained. While it would have been ideal to work with him on a lead line, the previous week he had a scare and ran off with the dreaded "draggin' rope" chasing him. She didn't want to risk his getting hurt, so she decided that the first round-pen exercise was the place to start. However, she would have to modify it to fit her circumstances.

First to get the feet to move. Considering the size of the pasture and other factors (did we mention that Odessa had to participate because she can't bear to be separated from Markiz?), this alone was a challenge. Donna decided to just ignore Odessa and concentrate on Markiz.

Donna kissed to Markiz and chased him with her body language; he turned and ran off; she turned away and backed off a few steps. He stopped. She chased him again; as soon as he moved, she backed off again. After a few tries, he was getting the picture — all she wanted was for him to move his feet when she told him to. For a spooky horse, this was easy. Of course, Odessa got moving, too.

Donna was careful to only use enough stimulation to get Markiz to trot. The fencing was not secure enough to risk asking him for an outside turn.

Then to get the feet to move consistently. This took the help of a second person due to the size of the pasture. Donna's friend had done some round-pen work and coached her.

Donna blocked off part of the long, narrow pasture so the horses didn't have a place to hide out. After a few minutes, Odessa dropped out of the game. (She thought it was fun at the beginning, but she sensed work ahead.) Donna got Markiz moving to the left and, with some effort, kept him going left. Every time he stopped or turned around, she just matter-of-factly kept him moving, mostly at a walk or trot. **An outsider watching would have thought he was trying to avoid being caught, as he**

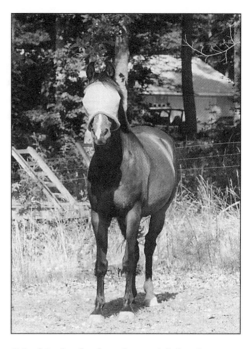

Markiz looked at her with both eyes. Even through the fly mask you can see the question mark on his face.

moved off each time she approached. In reality, she was making his feet move when she said "move."

After a few tries, Donna had Markiz making a big circle around her. She had him go about three times around, then backed off to allow him to stop. Again, three times around and allow him to stop. And again.

Had the fencing been secure, Donna would have gone on to the next round-pen step, an outside turn. But, with no outside fence to help the horse turn and as Markiz had never shown any signs of aggression, she moved right onto developing a cue to tell Markiz to come to her.

First, to get him to look at her. She patted her leg with her hand. Markiz looked (to see what was happening), and she turned and walked away. He stood there looking puzzled. She faced him again and patted her leg; he looked at her, and she stopped patting and turned away. This went on a number of times, each time Donna letting him look a longer time before she turned away. When she sensed he was about to turn away, she turned away first. If Markiz did not look at her, she made him move his feet and began the process again. At this point, he was about 30 feet from her.

When he looked away, Donna called his eyes back to her with the pat on her leg. If he looked, she stopped patting, talked to him, and let him stand there; if he didn't look, she made his feet move.

Little by little, they played the game, each time Donna moving closer to Markiz while he looked at her, then she turned away. Eventually she got right up to him, petted his nose and then walked away. It seemed to her that Markiz felt a sense of relief when she actually made contact with him.

Next, with Markiz watching her, she stepped to her right. He turned his head to follow her movement. **Donna's objective was to get him to "lock on her" with both eyes.** She did this several times, lengthening the time she asked him to look at her and the amount of bend in his neck. Eventually, she stepped right and he turned to face her. She stepped right again. He turned again. She turned and walked away, letting him know that was all she wanted.

Again, they did the dance, stepping right and then left, Markiz following her moves with his. She continued approaching him, petting his nose and walking away, stepping left and right, until she could walk in a circle while Markiz walked alongside as if on a lead line. They did this around the pasture and all the way down to the barn area. Then Donna petted him and left the pasture.

Lest you think it was all smooth going, we'll tell you there were a few glitches along the way. Odessa got into the act, and the mailman came by, both of which distracted them and had Donna going back to the beginning of the lesson. From Donna's perspective, the hardest part was keeping her concentration: **"It looks easy when you see it done, but watching the horse so you can turn away as soon as he's guessed the right answer is tiring. It was hard to know sometimes when to make him move or when to just call him again.**

"At one point when I was walking beside Markiz, he stopped and I walked on a few steps. I went back and petted him. He walked a few more steps with me and stopped. I walked on, then back to pet him. And again. My friend suggested Markiz thought I wanted him to stop, as I was rewarding his decision to stop by walking away, so I had to change what I was doing. When he stopped, I made his feet move. Then I asked him to look at me again. I walked up to him and petted him and we walked together. I stopped beside him to give him a chance to stop. After about three tries, he got the idea of staying with me, but it was emotionally draining for me. If I was having that hard a time figuring out what I

It was a challenge for Donna to keep Markiz' attention as Odessa, nearby, was a major distraction.

Looking at Donna for longer and longer periods, Markiz is about to move his feet in order to turn to face her.

A partnership begun, Donna used the mail (something readily at hand), to begin sacking out.

was rewarding, however inadvertently, imagine how hard it was for Markiz to know what I wanted.

"There were a few highlights. A time or two I could see him make a clear decision to look at me instead of messing with Odessa. That was neat. Another time I was stepping to the right and just wanted him to look at me and move his feet. He dropped his head and walked up to me. From that time on, when I patted my leg, he stopped and looked at me, then walked up to me. Those breakthroughs were really rewarding.

"I'm really looking forward to working with him again. Up until now, I thought he was pretty, but an expensive yard ornament. I can see that I may have been giving him mixed signals and that maybe he's not as silly as I thought he was; he just didn't know what I wanted. I had always assumed he was deliberately being difficult because he was spoiled. Working with him, I could see him making an effort to do what I asked. I need to remember that whatever I do, he's perceiving it as some kind of communication from me, even when I'm not intending to train him. I guess I'd better learn to be more consistent. After owning him four years, I think we're finally off to a good start." ▣

22

Training A Perfect Dog

*Since dogs and horses are both
conditioned-response animals, learning
to train your dog could help you train your horse.*

What do your dog and horse have in common? Oh, sure, they both have four legs, two ears and a tail. But more importantly, they are both conditioned-response animals. That means we can use the same type of training to adjust their behavior. Shirley Ruth Johnson trains dogs using the conditioned-response method, and she explains how you can learn horse-training techniques by training your dog.

Perfect Horse: *People can learn John's conditioned-response method for training horses by using it to train their dogs. Can you explain how?*

Johnson: When people teach a horse, it sometimes takes thousands of repetitions before they see substantial changes in his behavior. The trainer often worries that he is not doing the training correctly. So, he either thinks the horse is being stubborn, or he changes what he is doing, confusing the horse. Then, they both get discouraged.

Using John's conditioned-response training methods on a dog, however, the first training session produces visible results, and within six weeks, many first-time dog handlers have their dog obedient to all the basic commands, even off-lead. That not only gives someone a well-trained dog, but also helps the handler understand how to train, particularly how to use cues and to reward the dog when he does what the handler wants.

Anybody can learn to lead a horse the right way. With work, you can even train your dog to train your horse. The secret is in keeping slack in the lead rope.

PH: *Tell us about working with dogs.*

SRJ: Dogs understand the tone of our voice more quickly than the meaning of our words. Matter-of-fact tones are best for commands. Lowering your voice is unmistakably corrective. Praising him in a higher, happier tone will make it easy for your dog to know when you are pleased with his performance.

Neither dogs nor horses understand the concept of right or wrong. They think in terms of consequence. They understand pain, anger, fear, nervousness and other negative emotions. They also understand praise and enthusiasm.

Never dismiss it when your dog threatens, growls or glares — all serious aggressive signals. Your dog is not kidding, anymore than a threatening horse is bluffing.

The foundation for a companion dog is the same as for a top-level working or obedience dog, but the performance dog needs a thousand times more work on the same exercise. If you skip or hurry lesson steps, it will show up later as performance inconsistencies, which is what happens when training horses as well.

PH: *Tell us how your dog training parallels horse training.*

SRJ: To teach even the most simple command to our dog (horse), we need a lesson plan. The better the plan, the better the teaching, and the better the student's performance. The more steps we have in our lesson plan, the faster the student will learn.

We'll follow the same training rules as with the horses — you can't get hurt, the dog can't get hurt, and the dog should be better after the lesson than he was before. And, just like with those reins, you'll have slack in the lead 95 percent of the time.

Both riders and dog handlers must understand several concepts before they can solve problems. First, they are working with conditioned-response animals, which means habit-patterned or habit-forming. Secondly, they must use a logical cue system. Third, the trainers must be consistent in their repetition of these signals and their rewards.

PH: *Tell us about cues. Why would a dog not respond to a cue?*

SRJ: A cue is a specific signal that the trainer has taught. When "cued," the dog should respond to that signal within two to three seconds, 100 percent of the time. We use physical signals when training horses, then add voice cues later. With the dogs, we use hand signals and body language as the primary cue, and voice cues as secondary.

There are basically two reasons an animal doesn't respond correctly: 1) He does not understand what the cue means. If that's the case, the cue has not been taught well enough. 2) The dog understands the cue, but chooses to ignore it.

PH: *So, what do you do when the dog doesn't obey the cue?*

SRJ: Whatever the reason that the animal doesn't obey, the answer to solving the problem is the same: Return to a place in the dog's training where you can set up the conditions and get the response you want. Then build on that. Get the animal in the habit of cooperating with you. In dog training, as in horse training, the more steps you can put in the lesson, the quicker the dog will get the idea of what you want him to do.

Any time we ask the dog to change what he is doing, we need to know the answers to these questions:

1. What is the motivator? Attention, praise, petting, play or even food are good motivators for dogs.

2. What is the "yes" answer? What lets him know he did what you wanted? Praise. If his tail is not wagging, the praise isn't clear or strong enough. Figure out what is effective praise for your dog.

Consistent repetition is the key to success. But, consistency begins with the handler, not the dog. First comes the trainer's concentration, then the trainer's consistency, then the dog's performance, and finally, the dog's attention. Developing handler concentration is the single most difficult thing to do, and the most important. You have to learn to recognize changes in your dog and in his performance.

I try never to scold, but to encourage a dog, to keep him trying. Corrections range from a clean jerk-and-release of the lead to simply withholding praise. Good corrections are short and fast, letting the dog know immediately that he made the wrong choice, yet without creating any fear or distrust of you. If you cannot correct him just as he attempts the unwanted behavior, then don't correct. Set it up again, concentrating on getting the critical timing.

When he does the right thing, I make the dog feel like a winner by a show of enthusiasm. Set the dog up for success by giving him the benefit of the doubt. Praise him sincerely when he obeys.

PH: *How is the dog's lead like the horse's rein?*

SRJ: Always begin and end a correction with slack in your lead. It is impossible to give an effective correction with a tight lead. I see owners all the time who tighten up the lead even when the dog is in the right place doing the right thing, just as you see riders on a horse who's standing obediently still, but they still hold tension on their reins. What incentive does the animal have to repeat the good performance?

When you give the correction, grasp the dog's lead halfway down. As you reach for the lead and begin to take slack out, you are giving the dog time to respond before the correction is unpleasant. It's the same way when riding. The slower you move your hand on the rein, the quicker your horse will respond, because he wants you to put slack back in the rein.

PH: *What parallels do you see in working with a puppy and a foal?*

SRJ: There are many. You can begin training puppies at an early age, just as you can foals. Use their natural curiosity to your advantage by petting them and handling and picking up their feet, but releasing them before they try pull away. That way, you condition them to being held.

Shirley Ruth pats her leg — a pre-cue that tells the dog she is going to ask him to do something. We use pre-cues when riding, also. Our horse learns, for instance, that as we reach for the rein, we are going to ask him something. Patting one's leg, calling the dog's name and reaching for the rein all give the animal a "heads up" that a cue is coming and give him time to be ready to obey before the cue becomes an irritant. With consistent repetition, the dog (or horse) performs as well off-lead as on.

When you start teaching the dog to walk on a lead, ask for steps to the side, just as you teach a foal. So, if you pat your leg, call the dog's name, kiss and tug on the leash to the side, then reward him when he leans in your direction, you are on your way. If he pulls away, just hold the lead steady, but release on any movement toward you.

PH: *How does training parallel for adult dogs and horses?*

SRJ: Very closely. We teach both animals to watch us with both eyes. My dog sits with his eyes glued on me, waiting for a signal. In round-pen work, we teach the horses to look at us with both eyes.

The handling of the leash and lead rope are the same. We can't allow the animal to pull some of the time, like when we are just out for a walk, and then be surprised when he doesn't yield to pressure. We use the lead to keep the dog/horse from moving too far away from us, so we can give him the other cues, and also as a motivator. The dog/horse will learn to obey when you reach for the rein or rattle the collar as you reach down the lead. Some cues in handling the dog, just as when halter-training the horse, come from our body language. Even specific lessons parallel each other.

Training, not choking

Shirley Ruth recommends using an extra-heavy-duty large-link chain training collar. The bigger the links, the better. Large links make it gentle; its noisiness makes it effective. You can buckle it back with the leash snap when he's a pup, then use it as a slip collar when the dog is older. To select the proper size, measure around the widest part of the head, just in front of the ears. Add two inches to that measurement. Round up to the next even number. If the head measures 17 inches, adding two gives you 19 inches. Buy a 20-inch collar.

Putting on the training collar can be a mystery. Neither of the big rings fit through each other, so how is it supposed to go on? And which end do you pull from?

1. Hold the collar vertically so that the big end rings are on top and bottom.

2. Drop the chain through either of the larger end rings.

3. Slide the collar over your left arm and pull it tight. If it pulls taut from over the top of your arm, you could really give a big jerk and it would immediately release. Try a few snaps and see how hard you could pull, how much noise you can make, and how quickly it releases pressure. Now flip it around on your arm so the tension pulls from below, and you can see why it could be called a "choke collar." Jerk that, and you'll howl! No release — big pain!

4. Remove the collar from your left arm and place over the dog's head so that it pulls taut from above the neck instead of under the neck. Putting on the collar properly is the key to having it work effectively.

A training collar can be used only from one side. We are showing you how to set it up so it will work with your dog on the left. You will be training the dog from your left side. Notice how the ring that attaches to the lead comes from over the dog's neck when it is on correctly. When it is on wrong, the part that attaches to the lead comes from under the dog's neck, which means it cannot loosen after a correction.

Shirley Ruth explains to John that this collar is on her arm upside down. Even though there is slack in the line, there's no release. The training collar works similarly to the bit — the release is the key.

PH: *Can you give us an example or teach us something we can teach our dog, then our horse?*

SRJ: Sure. Let's teach the stay cue and the recall, or "come to me" cue. Both the dog and horse will learn to come to you more quickly if you have taught them to stay first.

Just as a point of reference, if you've watched John work a horse in the round pen, you know that he gets to a point in the training where he's going to teach the horse to come to him. He holds up a finger to signal "wait," and then he walks away. Then he kisses to the horse, telling him to move. The horse heads toward him. By telling the horse to wait first, John can tell him to come on cue.

Working with your dog, we'll assume you've already taught him to sit. Tell the dog to sit, then command him to "stay" by holding your open palm in front of his face, like a police officer directing traffic to stop. If he moves, pull straight up on the lead and repeat "stay." You will be standing face to face with him, so you can instantly correct him from this position. When he stays for a couple of seconds, return to his right side (the heel position) and praise the dog, ending one mini-lesson, just as John makes one "stay, then move" a mini-lesson.

If you think the dog will move in five seconds, return to your dog's side in four seconds and praise him. Then step sideways, then back to center. Step to the right and to the left, only a couple of feet away from the dog. This is especially important to an insecure or shy dog. Return to the heel position by walking around the dog from his left side to his right.

Do this at least 30 times. Step in front of the dog and then back to the heel position. You'll want your dog to be successful at first to build his confidence. Practice for a few seconds at a time. Even if it isn't much of a "stay," that doesn't matter.

Don't allow the lead to drag across the dog's face. You will be using your hand signal all the time you are teaching stay. Once he learns the basic concept of stay, you'll be able to increase the level of difficulty quickly.

When you can step a lead's-length from your dog, stand in front of him and say his name and "come." Make it a happy call. When he starts to move toward you, run backward several steps, gathering up the leash to guide him directly to your front. Give him the command to sit. If necessary, give the leash a quick jerk and release.

When he's sitting squarely in front of you, praise him. After he sits properly and you have praised him, give the signal and command to "stay." Go to your right, walking around the dog to heel

Just as when working with horses, we have to train the dog's mind, body and emotions. The dogs have to learn the cues, and practice them so they will respond correctly with any handler, despite myriad distractions.

position. Then give plenty of praise. Never scold or do anything unkind that he might associate with coming toward you.

PH: *Tell us how to do the same lesson with the horse.*

SRJ: Put the horse on a halter and lead rope, and treat the lead as a leash. Tell the horse to "stay" using traffic-cop body language, and step away from him. If he tries to follow you, put him back in position and tell him to stay quite firmly. Then turn to face him, kiss to him and pull the rope lightly. Hold tension until the horse begins to move toward you. Release the tension, and pet him. Just as you encouraged your dog when he made a move in the right direction, you'll want to do that with your horse. Just as with the dog, at first he may stay only a moment or two. That's OK; you can build on that.

If the horse doesn't move toward you when you ask him with the lead, you may have to get him moving by giving him the "go forward" cue on his hip. Once he's moving, put pressure on the lead, but then release it when he begins to turn his head toward you. Walk up to him and pet him. Then tell him to stay, and repeat the mini-lesson.

John tells the dog to stay. Note that he is looking at John with both eyes.

In no time, he'll be coming to you on cue.

When he gets really good on the lead rope, you can work up to a longer line, like a lunge line. Then, go back to a shorter line, but with distractions, such as another horse nearby. In time, you'll condition your horse to look at you when you kiss to him, and to walk toward you when you motion to him, as if he had a lead rope on.

PH: *You've said that the hardest part is being consistent. What do you mean by that?*

SRJ: The animal doesn't instinctively know what you want; he depends on the release to tell him. He also doesn't know when your signals count and when they don't count. So, he either takes them all seriously or ignores them all. If your horse ignores your cues, try teaching a similar lesson to your dog. The dog learns much quicker and is less intimidating than most horses. Any inconsistencies in your performance will show up faster with the dog. That will allow you to work through the lesson, or at least the concept of the lesson, and get your part down pat before trying to teach it to your horse.

And, best of all, if you make a mistake and teach the dog or horse to do something you don't want him to do, you can just replace the unwanted behavior with the behavior you want — just by using the conditioned-response method. It's fun. ■PH■

Index

For information regarding *John Lyons' Perfect Horse*,
the monthly magazine, see our web site www.perfecthorse.com
or call the publisher, Belvoir Publications, Inc. at 800-424-7887.

PHOTO CREDIT: MARK WALPIN, CHARLES HILTON, MAUREEN GALLATIN

BOOK DESIGN AND LAYOUT: SUSAN R. TOMKIN